TAKE

CHARGE

"Take charge"

ADETOPE ADENIJI

DEDICATION

The book is dedicated to God.

And also, to my beloved Mother and diamond that is worth to have forever, Late Evan.Mrs.Mary Aderonke Adeniji.

TABLE OF CONTENT

ACKNOWLEDGEMENT

My sincere appreciation to my wife, Tope Adeniji and my children, Tomiwa and Damola for the inconveniences I intruded on their path and the manner at which the vision was shared with me with broaden heart to attain success.

My appreciation goes to my biological father, The Very Rev.J.A.Adeniji(Rtd) and other parents, Sir&Rev. Mrs.A.B.Aladekomo, Daddy&Late mummy Ayo Oni, The Very Rev.&Mrs Ayo Richards, Daddy&Mummy Dipo Komolafe for the their parental administration and guidance.

My siblings, for being there for me even when seems there was constraints.

All the teachers of the world are recognized for their input to make me and to give me the key to my destiny.

Methodist Church Nigeria can not be excluded, being my church, a place of refuge, a place of prayers and supplication.

My schools are the best, thank you for the best you have made me to extract out of you.

However, to all my Christian, Muslim and other friends and readers, you are loved.

Thank you all, and God bless.

<u>INTRODUCTION</u>

There is nothing that was made without a specific purpose. The work of the creation was completed, comprehensive and well structured to the level of its optimal experimentation. There are many plain lands that have been able to generate different products and outcome without contribution of humans. All things are always working for a spectacular purpose, but the few who can realize its necessity have an advantage over others to convert them to various opportunities.

Just in the same way that plants and other resources are of use for different issues, so also are human beings in existence in relation to their significance. There is no one that does not have a specific reason to be created, but not all of us can interpret the work of existence as regards our full potential.

At the point of looking or thinking on what should happen in life, there must be consideration towards what should be the contribution of men to the necessary issues. Things are not meant to be made in their natural ways if the full expectation and results are the subject of the considerations of men. There must be injection of values that can structure life in accordance to the befitting taste that can make a greater impact.

Life is not fair to anyone, but can be fair to every one if due attention and consideration is given to relevant issues that can translate the activities of life to one's benefits. What we neglect to do is the chief cause of what we have not received or experienced. There is wide margin between what one can do, but fails to do, and that which one can not do. What makes what you can not do might not be far fetched from what you have considered not possible.

Counting on what people need to do for you or what you think they should add up to you might never be the greatest opportunity to lead you ahead or to make you. Looking around for someone to act on what you should do to step over a situation is never the golden key to success, but making oneself the major role in the activities that lead his or her ideas above and ahead.

Going to the market to get the ingredient to prepare a delicious soup is never the key issues to have it done. If all resources are well gathered or at the arm's length of a man, and yet he does not know the very best way to utilize the available resources, it might never result to anything. There must be direct involvement and control on the activities that lead to the predestined destination. There is need to give oneself to the activities that can bring forth the very best of his life.

Everyone knows what is good and bad for his status and his purpose, and this might never be evaluated in parallel with that of another man. What a man term to be success is never what another man counts to be so. This forms the basis of ones interest towards what the term success is referred. But the most interesting thing is that, to be a successful person in any way, you must be very prepared to have an adequate commitment that can lead you ahead of the others to be convinced that you are indeed successful.

It is a must for one to critically look into the situation around him to create a future of his vision, to be able to have something relevant produced through his efficacy and the contents he has within him. However, there is no way one can assume the stage of responsibility without being counted very significant to the related issues around his destiny.

You can only be responsible for your life when you know what responsibility means. There is every need to understand what a word or ideology means, to be able to dissect its real meaning and how it should operate, and how it is used, to be able to understand the main expectation on such words. Having concluded that the meaning of the word is expedient and very vital to be able to act or react accordingly, there is need to know or understand the real meaning of what the responsibility means before we can realize the meaning of the word and to have a full interpretation on the subject to be discussed further.

To be accountable means to be responsible, this means taking charge of an assignment and obligation. It illustrates that, someone is in charge of an event or activity which when there is any issues or needs to be resolved, such a man or individual is responsible for the outcome and the activities surrounding the whole scenario at which he is responsible. When one is in charge, it means that any liability and or obligation around the activity are rested on him. It is not stipulating the sense of belonging only, but also relating on the essentiality of being in control and responsible for any outcome and answerable to any issues relating to the obligation or duty.

Responsibility means a duty or obligation or liability for which someone is held accountable. It goes with the authority to be in charge, in control and to handle situation or issues as his own or as if he is responsible for the full details and outcome of the series of commitment and activities. It goes a long way to be responsible and to be in charge because it requires taking an action and attempts that can either emanate to the success or failure eventually.

Now that we understand what responsibility means, we can easily attribute its contents and ideology to correlate with having the responsibility to one's life. When one looks into the responsibility to one's life, the assignment seems to be more advanced than the former definition that have been made, in the sense that, without having a full responsibility of your life, it might be very tedious to have any meaningful responsibility in any other area of life. The urge to be responsible to your life or yourself gives the urge to keep on going extra miles to achieve a substantial worth of any meaningful purpose or assignment.

Life is so very precious and very crucial that it can never be handled with "I do not care" attitude, but with a meaningful and purposeful mind to make an head way. The series of the strategies that are however developed to make sense out of the numerous senseless activities are quite very important at the point of moving ahead and doing things that are exceptional and impactful. Being responsible for one's life means being responsible for the things that are necessary for the responsibility of the factors that can create fortunes and move one's life to the stage of no limitation.

When one knows what it means to be responsible for his or her life, he denotes the need to be very responsive and attune to those things that can make meaningful contribution to his purpose either knowingly or unknowingly. Without a personal contribution to the issues of life, life might never be worthwhile. There are numerous undertakings that are very pivot and essential to living that must be controlled before they bring forth their result. There are numerous values that are meant to be creating various opportunities, but they remain redundant as a result of having no influence on them.

Being responsible for one's life means that, one is able to deduce the need to be assigned the major need to have the full control of the issues around him and his projection and to be accountable for any outcome that comes therein. When one is responsible, he knows that no one is to be apportioned the fault of being a failure and ineffective other than the person himself.

Responsibility for one's life is a responsibility to all to make sensible and meaningful effects and to be fully part of the aspect of life that makes the uniqueness to ascend to the right destination. Without the full responsibility, there might not be accomplishment of purpose and the rightful placement of values. It is when one is fully responsible and in charge that he will understand that, it is very compulsory for him to try his best possible to accelerate on the option to expand his component to discharge things that are esteemed and of greater value to control the issues of life around him. There are some certain decision that are very compulsory and worthwhile to cause distinctive celebration and meaningful influence that can make the entire world to be beneficial of its effects, such disposition and coordination of purpose must never be left out to make a world of a champion through being responsible for his life.

When one is responsible, he understands better the very crucial need to define a life to its peak. He can see clearly what he is meant to be involved with to define living in a perfect way. Seeing beyond the ordinary to look into the issues that can make a better life and creating future for not only yourself, but to the lives of the others around you, to cause a betterment and improvement that will be living even after the exit of the initiator is what is referred to as being responsible in holistic for one's life. Without being responsible for one's life, there might be a complexity to understand what it takes to be responsible for the others. A responsibility that attracts only singular focus of idea or orientation to oneself is a refrained and restricted responsibility which might limit the area of encompass of the responsibility.

Responsibility is beyond being able to look ordinarily around what the immediate needs and desire look like, but the grace to be able to understand that there are diversified requirement for oneself to be able to give in the very best of his importance to move the world around and to be a catalyst to the increment and development that are very essential for the present and the future purpose. The desire to make a mighty impact is very crucial at the point of taking the decision that can take full charge of one's life. And before you can be in charge or fully in control of your life, there is every need to be able to be in control of the things around you. Things around that you take care either knowingly or unknowingly are the associated values that are responsible for the actualization and being in the full control of one's life either directly or indirectly.

Responsibility entails giving oneself in totality to what he has an insight on, and by this, one can say that, being responsible for oneself means an act of being able to see beyond ordinary to see the issues that are necessarily needed to be resolved to attain the full control of the inbuilt capability. It has to do with the related issues of the mind and the psyche to influence the world in which one lives. It has to do with what are the related effect of the unseen on the seen and how the translation occur freely through one's inbuilt creative ideas to take possession of what one has or anticipate to acquire.

There are responsibility that when they are left untouched or undone, might never allow destiny to be discovered or uncovered, such responsibility are the responsibility in association with what you can perceive that no other person can. What you can see and do is what can transform you largely, and these are the things that can make you to be the chief authority and in control of your destiny. The sincere aspect of life is that there is closely related attribute between having the control over the destiny and being in charge of one's life. You can never lose the opportunity of being in control of your destiny and you are in charge of you life. Being eager to have a full control over your destiny is what opens your internal personality to the realm of being responsible to one's life.

The issues of being responsible for one's life has to do with the concern of being self pushed other than being pushed by the external forces or individuals. One's willingness to be self motivated is quite very crucial and essential at the point of assuming the responsibility to be responsible for one's life. When one fails to be moved, he will be moved by the insignificant forces that should ordinary serve as a tool to the self attainment. When one does not know what to move him or her, he or she remains unconditionally stagnant to the irrelevances and the poorest of the result that should create advantage ahead of the others to be in control at the fullest realm.

However the subject of the book is to relate on the various issues that are supposed to be the embodiment of being in control of one's life, that is, the factors that makes one to be responsible for himself and to strife hard to connect with his proposed destiny. There are numerous of the points to be considered and looked into, but only few will be examined in the books at hand.

To then round it up, there is need to fight a good battle for oneself to be in absolute control and possession of his life. Being in control of oneself is absolutely necessary but it is never compulsory till personal definition is attained. Though, the subject is never compulsory, but it does not mean that it should not be well considered for the sake of the set of the individuals that might be willing to have a change or conversion as the case might be. Therefore, the issue of being responsible for personal definition and life can not but be over emphasized to encourage the innate man to be sensitive to the enlargement and expansion of the content that are relevant to the under must hijack destiny.

TOPE ADENIJI

+2348037184404

ABUJA, NIGERIA. WEST AFRICA

Chapter One(1)

<u>BE RESPONSIBLE</u>

Responsibility begins with those things that are meant to be done which you have given yourself ordinarily without compulsion to do them. There are numerous identifiable things that are meant to be done without forcing oneself to do them by the third party. The aspect of being careful of the harmful elements in one's surrounding is very expedient and necessary when one is looking into the scenario of being responsible to his life. There can never be life to be responsible to without taking care of it. Life is given freely by God, but it is one's duty and obligation to know that it must be well thoroughly taken care off to be able to accomplish vision and other projection of all kinds that the world might be demanding from the human nature.

One must be responsible to be exposed to knowledge and information. There are thousands of things that exist which can not be experimented or known without being massively informed. Information is the key to the progress and understanding of the needs of the issues around human nature. A man without information is a man without his sight to see or to know the need to move ahead. You can only get to know those things that you have the passion to do, and do things that you have considered very relative and important to be actualized. Information might never come ordinarily without the attempts that lead to it. One's mind is very important and quite very expedient at the point of consuming information that can be versatile and useful to his world. The sincere aspect of life is that, information can be living with a man without understanding or being in the light of it if one does not have interest to know about it. There might not be any need to move a inch as regards generating information that are necessary to life if one is wiling to have them accordingly to the age of the computer and technology.

One must be responsible to creating a career path for himself to accelerate his potency and capability to do exploit and to be able to measure up with the standard that is required to have a befitting life and a life that can make a result out of the activities of life. It is very possible to be sent to school, very possible to be enrolled for vocational jobs and other things that can create avenue for the opportunities of life, but it is never possible to force a man to become what he is meant to be if sincerely he wants to be it. Without seeing the reason for you to be effective and functional in the aspect of life you have considered as a human, there might never be any circumstance that can give you the result you need or expect as a result of not being willing to effectively discharge your responsibility. What I am saying is that, as human, you must be willing and aspire to connect with your future without any one pressurizing you to doing so. You have the responsibility of making a life that can meet with the need of your future. A reasonable man should know what he needs and wants for himself to ascend to the stage of no limitation and to be outstanding among his peers. He should have something so genuine to compete with steadily to make a simple impact in his environment and the world to be remembered when he is no more.

There is another responsibility that is very crucial and necessary, that is the responsibility of consuming the right diet foods and edible substances. What is light as regards this, each individual is held responsible for the nature of the consumption of the contents or substances they consume. The thinking faculty must be able to control the internal man to have a gauge or limitation to the things he consume or do. A good multivitamin is required for development and growth, so, they must be prepared and made available for the intention of consumption to maintain a good and healthy living. In as much as this is not a religious book, I will only say that, there should be limitation for all forms of consumption among which are, cigarette, alcoholic drinks, cola, soft drinks, eating habit, e.t.c.

Being responsible for the creation of the pattern of the family of one's desire is one of the most important aspects that one must be responsible to do. One must not operate under the influence of the others to have a family of his interest or choice. In the time past, we have series of diversified issues among which are, mandating a man to marry a woman, mandating a man to have a specific number of children, compulsion of the nature of the house or accommodation that one should have before getting married, castigating the wives that can not give birth to a male child till they are set packing, e.t.c. A man should never give the direct control of such activities to the people around him, but rather to have a full influence on what his perception and responsibility are. Different people with different ideas and different ways of life and characters to accomplish the same intention and purpose, if you are responsible for your life, you should be able to decide on how to build your life, how to structure your intention as regards the family related instances and the number of children to have should be sorted out with your wife not any other person. However, the family issues are very sensitive and should be handled by the people that are directly involved in such activities, that is, husband and wife.

Responsibility cut across the nature of life that one is willing to have in the aspect of making his little contribution to the existence. There is always a connection between what you have to give and how you take care of your life. To be responsible for your life means that you are fully in charged to make a meaningful impact, aside this, no meaningful or genuine accomplishment can be made. Giving the best to achieve the very best at the point of moving ahead is worth while to be mentioned while looking into the area of being in custody or in charge of his or her life. To be responsible means that you are always very conscious of the fact that, you must be spent to extract values that are in consistent and of the same nature with what can propel you to have an equitable evaluation to the responsibility.

Before now, I mentioned information as a key thing, but there is every need to know more about that. The nature of the information that are accessed are numerous among others, this can be constructive or destructive in nature. There is every need to prune one's thought and information that can be accessed to be able to have a well refined thought that can translate to the advancement and increment in the standard nature of the world. It is the responsibility of the human being to have access to the information around them and at the same time, to be able to determine which of the information should be acted on or ventured into to command the fruitfulness of the world. Either developmental or destructive, each individual are responsible to have a decision on the nature of the information to receive and how they should be converted to the values of their choices. However, to be in alignment with the structure that can yield a fruitful outcome on the responsibility of the human to their nature of lives, there must be full consideration on the processing, assessment and utilization of the information within the context of the human deliberation.

Something similar to this particular point was made while deliberating on the responsibility to have a choice of family. I was trying to say that, under no circumstance should any one allow any external force to put him or her under the compulsion of determining where to stay or the nature of house to reside. Here, I am trying to look into the elaborate aspect of the vicinity and area or region, and country of residence.

Many people have formed their respective decision or formulated their respective mind set based on the nature of the theoretical word around them. Many have moved to different areas or country without any basis than due to the admonition from the friends and through other sources. Candid speaking, there are a lots of the individuals that are suffering bitterly as a result of the advise they acted on wrongly, while few are so lucky that, the nature of the advise that did not work perfectly for someone works easily for them. In any way, I am of the school of thought that, each individual should be able to determine their area of choice of living without compelling them to doing so. Candid speaking, this has a tremendous weight on the issue of responsibility to one's life. And sincerely, it must be well treated and given the full consideration to have an absolute control on the nature of one's life.

Though, we have series of clues that lead to the full responsibility of one's life, but to be able to move ahead, I will like us to have a curtail of expression, but before I round it up, I will like to discuss on the issue of saving and investment. These two words are very important to existence, and sincerely it might mean series of definition to a man or other. The percentage that is kept on all inflow or any related economic function or gift or benevolence that are not spent immediately is termed to be savings. There are a lots of argument on either to have it removed before the actual fund is being spent or the left over on the money. Which ever way, what one keeps as result of the money received from all daily commitment or through gift is called savings. On the other hand, investment can be personal development and learning of skill and jobs, it can be investing money or fund on the activities that can yield future result, such as debentures, shares, bonds, investment on a business, investing on land and landed properties, education investment, vocational investment, e.t.c. The major point here is that, issues related to this cause should be willingly undertaken. There might be counsel or teachings on them, to realize the need to have them in place, but sincerely there is no justification for any of these to be imposed on any one. However, the result on this forms part of the issues that leads to the responsibility of one's life, and must be well sensitively handled and related on to make a better way into one's glory.

Chapter Two (2)

<u>BE AN ACHITECT AND A CONSTRUCTOR</u>

Life is real and those who live in it must make it real. There is nothing in life that does not entail thinking it or sketching it out before becoming real. Genuine and unique men are made based on their nature of the vision they caught up with and how they put them into their various use. Going back to the work of the architect or constructor, most often, they take their time to critically border their inner value to views beyond the physical to plan for how a structure or construction work should be. Before the commencement of the building, that is the physical building or construction work, there is always building at the apex degree of the order in the intellectual realm and on the paper that simply reveal the true nature of the expectation of the reality.

One might not achieve anything or achieve little without having a concrete planning and full design of the nature of life that one wants to live. At the point of the creativity and innovation, people are driven with what they can see or perceive at the realm higher than ordinary. One might not be able to accomplish any meaningful thing without the preparation to take possession and to make it real. And sincerely, everyone has the capacity to see their various values and ideas independently in order to create what is identifiable to their concepts which might be closely related to what another man has, but can never be similar.

Just same way that the physical projects are embarked on, the architectural and construction potency are made and configured. This means that being an architect or constructor of your life can lead you to be involved in the work of creativity and innovation which can be demolished and adjusted to one's desire when due. The usual saying of a man is an architect of himself is proven in the point of the consideration under the subtopic just related on.

To be responsible for your life, there is always the need to see beyond what you can see. There is no one that can not see something spectacular, but not all can see them when they are not formed or make themselves to see things that might not ordinarily be seen. As a man or human that aims at making provision for responsibility, there is need to be vast to the level of being able to see beyond ordinary in all circumstances to understand the need to be an architect or constructor of life. To have a fulfilled responsibility, there must be fulfillment of seeing beyond the normalcy.

Another vital point in association with having the full responsibility is having the creative mind or being a creator. Creativity has to do with the creating of values and intention that can make advantages to the existence. It has to do with what can be seen at the realm higher than physical to make a direct fulfilling imagination coming into reality. Every one has all what it entails to see and to convert them to the possibilities of life. The aspect at which what can be seen is processed to the finished point is termed creativity. Creativity is the mother of all innovation and logics behind every advancement or improvement. However, being creative is quite very essential at the point of making a responsibility for one's life. If at all you have seen logic or thought that is in existence, worth to be emulated, there is always the need for the creativity to function in such a way as to make a better valuable one other than just its replica. Making a responsible life can never be separated from the angle of being very creative to bring about innovation and advancement.

Being an architect means that you need to be substantial and expedient in your thought, this means that, you must have surplus of information and elements that are very relevant to the issues in relation to the growth and development of the world. Before one can assess series of information or come forth with the substantial ideas around his thought, he must be able to assess the right information to the developmental purpose, he must be productive in his in-depth extraction of power of thought, and be a converter of the information to values. One must be very substantial and expedient in his thought to be able to attain the stage of no limitation and to access the stage of responsibility.

Several things have been said, but this aspect is relating on being a worker of miracle. There are a lot of things that are very necessary to be involved in the processing that lead to miracle. Creating an avenue for miracle means creating an avenue for astonishing and amazing doings and experimentations, as far as I am concerned, miracle can not happen without having the believe in it. You must be able to see the miracle happening and be very set to have an encounter with them before you can access them. Miracle might be defined with things that have to do with your faith, believing that they are accomplished before they are embarked on. This can only be translated to the full grown miracle when you have the fullest assurance that they are accomplishable and attainable. One can then say that, to be a miracle worker or experience miracle, one might never be able to do away with the elements that lead to it. This then lead us to the necessity of being a miracle worker to have a total control of the resources within one's capacity and to be well responsible for one's life.

Thinking positively is quite very essential at the point of attaining responsibility in line with being an architect or constructor. Positive thinking is the maker of the positivity and productivity. One must never give his heart to the things that are not positive in nature, what you can perceive has a greater role on what you will do or act on. The idea of positive thinking is a structure that leads to accessing the realities of life and acting on them accordingly to generate result or have a meaningful impact. Without thinking positively, there might not be any meaningful justification on the things that are right or wrong. There might not be an avenue for the greater logics that can lead the world to its apex level. There might never be decision to act in a specific direction or the other to make a sensible effect. A man or human must have the right thinking to be able to understand the need to have a certain purpose or the other accomplished, and sincerely, everyone has the capability of thinking rightly to be in charge and in custody of his or her life, or to be responsible for it.

Being an architect or constructor means that one must be someone that can appreciate things around him. Without having the mind to appreciate what you can see or access in life, you might never be able to understand the importance of the existence of such intention or thing. Thinking vigorously has to do with appreciating the value and the intention behind the available activities and contribution to the advancement of the world. Being appreciative makes a man to have a critical desire to and urge to be part of the reformation or improvement that might be demanding in the nearest future. Without understanding of the things that are in existence, you might never be able to understand the need to have amelioration on them to create better befitting benefits. We can not discuss on construction and architectural work of the responsibility of one's life without looking into the aspect of being an appreciative minded individual.

To be a constructor and architect of one's life, there is need for one to be able to freely give from the source, which means that, one should be able to give what he has freely from within without anyone forcing him or her to do such. Architectural and constructional work is the evidence of the abundance of the mind and the right attitude to be freely given. The diversified resources within the mind are the structures that embodied the construction and architectural work. Without being a cheerful giver, you might not really know the implication of being an architect or constructor of one's life. So also, without being able to construct one's life, there might never be an avenue to be in charge of the constructive works that control the logics behind its responsibility.

Knowing about the needs and desire of the people is very essential at the point of making an head way to the success of the construction and architectural work of creating responsibility. There is no way a responsibility can be assumed when there in no clue of what are the things that are relevant to existence. One might not just ordinarily assume responsibility without knowing that which he needs to be responsible. To be responsible means understanding the aspects that is essential to be responsible for. If a man does not know what he is responsible to do, it might be very complex for him to realize the actual area of his necessity and functionality toward his responsibility.

Each individual is meant to check on the aspect at which their responsibility can be of need, and to know how to come into making them attended to accordingly. Having no thought or clue on the need and the desire might never fetch a good result or come forth with what it entails to be actually responsible for the issues of life. What I am trying to enumerate under this point is the aspect of knowing and showing concern for the needs around a man before being able to identify the actual place of his need to be well responsible for the full control of his life. There is always the need to know where to function and what to function on before realizing what should be done which lead to responsibility. One must have the full detail of what it entails to make a meaningful contribution which pave way for his responsibility.

Learning and acquisition of knowledge and upgrade might never be over emphasized to have what it entails to construct effectively. The necessary exposures that are relevant to the forwardness and development of the whole contents of life are very keys to make the right decision that can build up responsibility. One must never be at ease without learning or adding value on daily basis. The information accessible and acquired knowledge are very vital at the point of coming forth with the high

standard of responsibility. This very point is quite very
pertinent and worth to be noted to have all it takes to
be set and fully ready to make a thorough decision
that leads one ahead. Education is very relevant and
quite worth to be noted to define what responsibility
means, and to be able to maturely be involved. When
one does not know what responsibility means, he
might never depict the need to be responsible in any
way. The level of the responsibility that one makes
himself to be involved with has to do with the level of
learning or exposure that is available to him. There is
need to be eager to learn and to add more value to
oneself to be able to see the necessary need for him or
her to be out-rightly responsible. However, to be
responsible for your life, there might be all need to be
well exposed and fully in the light of the essence of the
education and all other form of learning that
necessitate a perfect construction and architectural
work.

The ability to be resilience and toughed in nature is
another main element to be able to have a
construction and architectural work that are worth
while to lead one into being fully responsible for his
life. The potential effect of being resilience means that,
one is composed of what it takes to be alive when
there are distortion and impediments. This is an act of

moving ahead irrespective of the odds and the unwarranted forces that are meant to exterminate vision, purpose and projects. The issues here is that, one develop the attitude of standing or re-standing in the midst of the forces that are meant to cause extinction in one's view and foresight. A man must be very toughed and extremely resilience to be able to handle the various challenges of life. The challenges of life must come to our ways, but there is always the need to be in control of the activities that might be willing to obstruct the view. In nut shell, to be in full control of oneself, there is need to be constantly resilience and toughed to suppress the devourer of vision. Without being in control, there might never be the situation of being in the control of one's life.

Another point that is worth noted is the ability to be self motivated and personal teaching. Apart from the exposure and teaching through upgrade that was mentioned before, there is a very huge necessity to learn on how best one can as well teach himself or motivate himself to do a certain thing or the other. Self motivating and teaching are always very voluntary and with the fact that they are voluntary, it paves way for the best of the option to see better and clearly at the point of discharging responsibility. What I am saying is that, human being is capable of carrying out structural researches and findings that can be very pertinent to existence when they pay attention to the need to be self motivated or teach themselves. There are numerous opportunities around human nature that can cause transformation, and, or be a catalyst to the functionality of the maximum operation of life, and not until these series of the element are touched, tapped and made to be of value to life, they might be passive and unproductive in nature. Therefore, to be amounted to be an individual that can have a perfect architectural work or construction, there will be need to be a self teaching and self motivating being. This however translates to the instance of responsibility, and having the true control of oneself.

There is always the need to participate in the development purpose. A developmental efficacy minded must be very inclined to the nature of moving around the series of the instances that can lead to the multiplication of worth and value that can lead the world ahead. Being developmental is quite very essential to be able to tap into the region of being widely connected with the pattern of architectural and construction work that can produce unquestionable result. One must have something he can see, and what you can see must be very adequate to be seen to deal with the issues of life. Without the presence of the element that can expose a man accordingly to the true nature of life issues, there might never be any developmental purpose in connection dealing and undertakings. When one has the urge to be fully involved in the things that are developmental, he forms the entire content within what he can do or act on around that which is visible to him. Being developmental is essential to being efficient to construct an impartational qualitative function that can affect the generation, which however resolved to the issue around being responsible in a matured manner to take responsibility in life, and also to be responsible for one's life.

In this segment, my intention is to look into the issues that are very necessary to make a perfect architectural work and construction that can build the courage to have a full responsibility to one's life.

Chapter Three(3)

<u>ACCEPTANCE OF FAULT AND NOT SHIFTING OF BLAME</u>

One of the major concern to be well noted at the point of looking into the aspect of life that leads to the full responsibility of life can not but be emphasized in the region of the acceptance of one's fault and shifting no blame to the others. Often at times, we often shift blames irrelevantly or fail to admit our faults. There is need to be very truthful to ourselves as regards the issues of having responsibility in the result or effect of what happen to us. There is every tendency of being able to learn on whatever that transpires and to be able to resolve such incidence in the nearest future. Being very set to accept fault is very necessary and quite very essential in life to assume the stage of responsibility. There is no way one can live his or her life without issues around it. The nature of issue that comes up from an angle or from an individual is quite very different from the nature of the issues that emanates from another man, but the most important thing is that, there is no kind or nature of issues that can not be well analyzed and resolve.

When issues that are meant to be the substance to the developmental purpose are disowned or neglected, they become the issue that when next they occur, they are terror and more lately, destruction. What I am saying is that, any issue experienced should be an issue to learn from, not an issue to run away from or to count as another person's responsibility. Learning on handling issues makes a man to be prepared ahead of the issues. Men that are often in expectation of issues are better placed to give a resounding remedy. Therefore, it is quite very expedient for each individual to be well set to accept all nature of the problems or issues that might tend their ways.

Issues erupt everyday and they come in different way and nature, the issue that is applicable to someone might never be the issue that is relevant or that someone of the same nature of activities experience. Issues come in diversified ways and they are always having what should be the solution to them around them when one is fully set to handle them. To someone, having drinkable water is his challenge while to another man, being able to eat is the nature of the issue he experiences. Each day has its issue, and the nature of the issues around a day which are similar might not need a similar remedy to have a lasting solution to them. These issues are however supposed to be well analyzed and to be resolved other than shifting the blames or faults to the others. One must be responsible for the associated problems around him to be able to get to the level of being bold enough to have all what it entails to be responsible for his life.

It was stated ahead that there is no issue that can not be resolved, but all resolvable issues depend on what one has in mind and how he or she has seen the problems around him. As it was said, there is no issue of any kind that is new any more under the heaven, but they tend to make themselves available in different ways and how they happen. Therefore, if some of the issues around have been resolved in one way or the other, it means that they can be resolved again and again, but the main point remains that the tactics to each of them are quite very differentiated from one another. To then develop the attitude of resolving the issues around, one must be connected with the responsibility stage of life. Most of the issues are left unresolved when people could not have any form of justification to resolve them. The resolvable issues are the issues that are made to function as if they are resolved before they are given the necessary empowerment to be resolved. So, to be responsible for one's life, the sub topic at hand is quite very essential.

To have a solution to the issues around oneself, there is need to have the impression of resolving the issues before they are found the relevant solution. One must possess the mind of having remedy to the problems. What this means is that, problems should not be counted as one, but as issues. The problems around form the greatest tenet to teach on the full expansion and reasoning around becoming enlarged in the mental content to force out the internal genius to carry out the function that are exotic and gigantic.

Another important factor that must be well analyzed and cross examined at the point of resolving issues by accepting the fault and not shifting blames is making the issue to be friend other than being the enemy. Issues have been from the time immemorial, and they will continue to be part of the activities that will formulate the whole activities in the world forever. Issues are meant to be well handled, and to be accepted or taken to be friend to human at the point of handling them. What I am saying is that, one might never be able to resolve issues without having the closed relationship or contact with them. You can only see the perfect remedy or avenue to the rectification of the problems only when you can have an adequate relationship with such identified circumstances. To therefore be responsible for one's life, there is very need to be friend to numerous issues around, because this can only serve to be an avenue to actualize decision that can lead to a betterment of the nature of the future.

Having the mind of knowing that what create issues today are the relevant circumstances that can lead to the betterment of the future is quite very essential. Not to be someone full of shifting faults and blames to the other people or factors surrounding him, there is always the need to be very possessive of the mind that silently mention it out to one that the issues around should be the best tool to make the solution of tomorrow. To then have what it is to be moved to achieve the totality of being in control of personal life or being fully responsible, there is need to have the mind set of understanding the issues now are the direct or indirect way of creating tomorrow.

At a point before now, I mentioned of being a friend to the issues that emanate from any of the circumstances around a man. This particular point is the continuation of point above. One might never be able to have close study or thorough study of the identification of a problem when such problem is not well related with. You must have a full connection with the situation that leads to any issue that connect with your destiny as a human, and you must never look at the issue to be something that can not be resolved. Making an attempt to make issue friends or to closely peruse them makes the issues to be well studied and to make decision that can gainfully exterminate the odds. To have a responsibility that is of high value to be in charge of one's life, there must be connection between one and what he passes through to make a relative solution and remedy.

Sincerely, if I should say praying for issues is one of the greatest prayers that a man should offer on daily basis, many would look at my thought being foolish. There are some foolishness that gives room for the better life and amelioration of one's condition. Though, one should not forget that, the due diligence to be a champion of such issues should at the same time requested. Issues are the sources of the expansion in the thinking faculty of a man, and sometimes, not until they are experienced, mind and the best human composition might never be in its best use. They make the reasoning to be widened and create a new logic and thought that can meet with the situation at hand. Therefore, as human, there is every need to have an expansion in the thought through what he or she passes through to be able to live above the creation of the fake flimsy excuses that have been the enemy to the development of the world. In whole essence, to be in full control of the responsibility around one's life, there is always the need to be very conscious of the need to be expanded and improved on the logics that lead to a greater purpose which can only be generated through how best issue erupted can be handled.

To be availed the full privilege and advantage to be in full control of one's life, a man must be willing to spend time on the issues he undertakes. There is no magic to the solution of the issues without expending time on such issue. The time available for you while experiencing an issue or the other should not be invested on the irrelevances or looking out for the creation of the flimsy excuses, but rather to be judiciously spent on the avenue at which lasting solution can be generated or created. Looking at changing your job or starting something expedient might be an issue to you. My logic is that, we need to invest time on whatever we may need to do to get over them. The responsible sets of individuals are the responsible minded that can control their time and make provision for the time to reason on the factors that can rightly place them at their places of expectation.

A man must see the possibility in the impossibility to be able to move with faith to have remedy to the issues around him. When one works with bare sight, he can only figure out what he can see or that others have seen. But when one works with faith or inner sight, he sees beyond ordinary. There is need for the formulation of the possibilities around someone's thought before he can attain the degree of accepting the fault and looking forward to the solution thereof. Seeing the possibility in the midst of the impossibilities means that, all what you access at the point of relating or dealing with the issues around your consciousness is the direction to the accomplishment and achieving the perceived impossibilities. There is every need to be able to access the possibilities in the issues that are in connection with life before they can be fully accomplished. There is no doubt that, to be responsible for one's life, there is always the need to know what the possibility means, and to know how to arrive at the possibilities around the situations of life.

Being responsive to the action that leads to the solution of the problems or issues in relation to life is quite very essential and worth taking to be responsible for one's life. Not to forget our area of concentration as regards the point we are trying to study, we are looking into the area of accepting fault and not shifting fault in the context of being responsible for one's life. To have a lasting solution that can make a new life or solution to the numerous issues that might be tormenting one's life, there must be an action that can lead to the solution ground of the unwanted circumstances. To be responsive means to be reactive and quickly move towards something. This means being responsive to the issues means that, being able to react or quickly move toward having a solution to the issues. Someone that does not want to be defrauded of his or her ambition must be reactive to it. You can not just sit down complaining and think that things will be in order. There must be an activity that is connected to the formation of one's solution to any issue he might found himself to have a solution. Therefore, being responsive is quite very relevant and pertinent to constantly be in charge of one's life or responsible for the associated values in relation to life.

Being responsible for one's life has to do with the clarity of purpose or being able to define the condition around his life as the greatest advantage to attain the best fortunes. Without being formulated with the contents that makes the total scenario around one the best of the advantages to move to accomplish purpose, he might not be able to live over the issues living with him. I have talked on the issues of today being the solution for tomorrow and more other informational thought. But without being able to see the issues around you as an avenue to the greatest height or such that leads you to your fortune, you might never be able to realize the huge necessity to be advantaged or be accorded the greatest possibilities in the issues created around destiny, and to be frank, this is an imminent part of the value that turns out to be the option for the responsibility of life.

Chapter Four(4)

<u>ADJUSTMENT</u>

One of the most crucial points that is very mandatory at the instance of making a move to be responsible is the issue of adjustment. There is no one that can not adjust to the situation around him or her but the very complex of all things to do in life is adjusting to the issues around him. The major detriment to the regularization of the issue of life is the inability to adopt and adapt to the relevant changes. Being responsible means the ability to change equally to the things that can bring about the stability and improvement in one's life, environment or thought. As said before now, there is no issues that can not be fetched the lasting solution if one is well set and fully ready to act accordingly on them. I will be delighted to relate on the adjustment in relation to the responsibility of one's life through the analysis and elucidation on the points that follows.

What does adjustment means? It can be fine tuning a certain issue for its best outcome. It can be changing part or whole lots of the system that brings about an instance to be able to have a better performance or qualitative result. It can be said to be an alteration of a project, process, procedure, e.t.c to have a specific outcome of one's interest. It can be said to be modification of the whole or part of a function to have a prepared outcome or result. It might be said to be a regulation that makes one to behave in certain way or speedily upgrade his disposition to meet with the standard. It may be assumed to be the correction made on a certain action or reaction that leads to certain event. And lastly, one may look at it as an amendment on a specific activity to measure up with the level of its expectation.

The definitions given are enough to introduce us to the full meaning of the adjustment and to have a full meaning of what it is expected of its nature to assume the stage of personal responsibility.

However, what are the situations that are meant to be adjusted? There is always the need to have adjustment in life. There are always things to be adjusted and amended on daily basis as a result of the imperfection in the related issues around. One of the things that are very relevant to be adjusted can not be far fetched from the issues in relation with how one relates with the others. Relationship with the others is one of the key factors that are very crucial to be examined at the point of assuming the stage of full responsibility. No one is an island of knowledge, and no one is competent enough to live in life without having a perfect relationship with the people around him. There is always the need to be very sensitive to the issue of relationship at the point of looking into taking the position of authority and being in control of life.

Financial spending must be well treated and analyzed to be able to have a maximum control of one's life. Most people live above what they can generate before they generate them. Sincerely speaking, issues in relation with finance has a long way of affecting humans in either positive or negative way, and must be well treated and analyzed to be able to have a responsibility in the issues of life.

Adjustment in the way one consumes various substances that are meant to be the contributor to the growth and healthy living; With the fact that these sets of the consumable substances are meant to be relatively of advantage to the human in term of their health and condition, when they are well controlled and consumed rightly, it is better for the health responsiveness to better condition and living.

Sleeping or wastage of time can be very dangerous and devastating if not properly schedule. Time must be well managed and treated fairly. It is essential for one to sleep when due and to relax, play around with the friends and relative, but it will never be too reasonable not to know how to have a gauge or full control on the things that can keep or waste one's time. There must be schedule for all things, the time to sleep must be well cross examined, there is no one that does not feel like sleeping from time to time, but one must be able to have a maturity control that is essential to be able to accomplish a spectacular function. Also, the issue of relating with the people or catching fun with the others is also relatively important, but must as well be adjusted to be able to have a fulfillment of purpose.

Another adjustable situation that relates with being responsible for life is the control of expenses. One must be able to be in charge of the expenses he gets involved with. There should be saving culture and investment planning to meet up with the issues in the time to come. One should be able to think of what can make his condition growing and flourishing without impairment or difficulties in the time to come. Issue surrounding savings and investment are relatively very essential when one considers the ownership of one's life.

What dress should be put on, what should I say, where
should I go, what nature of the set of individual should
I have as friend, what nature of the economic function
do I do, where should I stay, what kind of the course or
discipline should I do in the institution, who should I
be married to, how many children should I have, what
are the choices around one's perfect living, time to
pray, what do I have to give to the world, how do I give
what I have, what are the things that I can do, how do I
affect the people around me, e.t.c, are the set of the
questions that must be resolved to be able to
understand what responsibility means in the whole
essence of life. A perfect question must be given and
available to these questions to be able to gain the full
control that is relevant to the state of being able to
have full knowledge on what a man should do to have
a full control of his life.

To then look at the mind that can be attuned to
adjustment, one needs to look at the mind that is
responsive and that is willing to make use of the
greatest advantage around it. It must be a life that
knows the essence of living, a life that can interpret
the situation to its best efficacy, humble mind, mind
that can think straight in all situations, a mind that
knows that values not revealed to him is as well
essential to its developmental concern, a mind that

can see possibilities always, a mind that knows what it entails to make a simple contribution to the world issues, a mind that recognizes the reality of life, e.t.c are the nature of life that can be attuned to the adjustment. There is no one that can not be regulated or attuned in the scope of life, but one must be delighted in the characteristics of the elements that are noted for the adjustment to take place.

What is termed adjustment can be seen or handled in different ways, it can manifest in diversified manners. What I am saying is that, adjustment can either be positive or negative in nature. It can lead to the destruction of the initial values and conditions before having a better nature, it can as well lead to the impairment of the value on ground before it can have another shape of its intention, and sometimes, it leads to starting afresh. One should be able to have the mind set ahead of the adjustment that, these natures of the elements that are sometimes not very friendly might be the subject of the affliction around the adjustment to attain responsibility in life. I am only trying to say that, adjustment is quite very essential at the point of assuming a standard responsibility. Getting to one's destination might require various tactics and systematic approaches. Therefore, the issue of adjustment is as relevant as the issue that emanated

the view to have a purpose and concern in life.
Therefore, having a full preparation for the best and
planning for the best is one of the most essential needs
to have an edge way in life, and these are in
association to the attainment of the responsibilities.

No matter how toughened or complex the adjustment
that one encounters looks like, they are always
towards the related issues of reformation and
improvement. The point is that, at the point of
enrolling for a particular program or course of study, or
making the attempt to under study someone as
regards learning or acquiring new skill and knowledge,
there is always necessity to have impairment on the
things that one does or engages with as a result of the
time to be devoted or concentrated on the new
intention. Something must be directly or indirectly off
you before another stage of life can be attained. Such
is the issue of adjustment that leads to the phase of
having a full responsibility of one's life. The whole
essence of the settings are to create the best options
to the avenue that can bring about result and
opportunity to making a better nature of standard of
life that should be channel towards the real ownership
of destiny.

Another importance of the adjustment is sighted in its attempts and discoveries of better standard of living. Adjustment is meant to create a situation that can ameliorate the disorderliness in the nature of living. It is an avenue to check for the best option when it is the time of the decision on the kind of life one wants to live. When one can adjust, it gives the best advantage to be able to blend up with the situations and to cross examine the best of the varieties that can be implemented or chose to have the best type of the living. The nature of life that one lives is very essential at the point at which one is looking into how he can be fully responsible for his life. And sincerely, it is better to be adjusted and well regulated to make a preparation for the apex degree of the concentration that can avail human the unlimited factors to the full control of the inbuilt and innate genius to make an unquestionable contribution to the existence, and without this, there might never be an avenue to full control to one's life.

When one looks into paving ways for the unseen opportunity, one is looking at the observation of the series of avenue to fortunes. Many people assume that they are not fortunate even when the fortunes around them should have created to them a larger world. Adjustment makes the world to know that, a particular place you are is not the very best place you are to be or to determine that many other function can still be coagulated to formulate the best decision around your destiny. Without seeing the opportunities around your destiny, you might never be able to know the need to tap into them to construct a very enviable decision that can affect the entire world and make difference in your life. What a man sees matters at the point of stepping into the action that can affect his destiny. Since the book is looking at being responsible for one's life, this particular instance is quite very relevant to understand that, every one are very opportune to create a bigger factors that should make a better outfit of their destiny. To be responsible then for one's life there is utmost need to be able to see the impossibilities very possible to make the whole factors working around one's destiny very friendly and lucrative towards making decision that can translate failure to the greatness. There is no way one can be responsible without being able to see clearly of the unseen factors around him to create what people might never assume to happen. Things that are happening are the things that are normal and that have been seen, but things that are unseen and yet to be demonstrated are the things you can see but yet to do. Learning on the acting on the things that can be seen but unseen by the others can be the best option to making thorough responsibility in life.

Adjustment can be attributed to the act of relating on the present issues without any rigor and anticipate to have the best outcome in the events that are yet to be attained. When one possesses the nature to be regulated in the midst of the challenges and difficulties, he is always seeing the need to convert shortcomings to the creation of series of the diversified advantages. To be able to adjust is what makes difference in your presence and definitely your behavior in your time to come to excel. The set of the challenges that are erupting or coming up from time to time are such that are very expedient to learn from at the moment of adjustment to be able to move on. Adjustment often gives different trials or attempts to overcome. This is as a result that, the more you adjust, the more you see the need to adjust in the subsequent issues or related issues of life. Being adjustable is an attitude that is common in the life of the champion, and that is the reason that the champions are always in connection with the things that adjust the world and adjust them. To wage into the situation at hand and in the future, there is always the need to have all what it takes to have due adjustment and to understand that adjustment is the prerequisite to the betterment of the nature of life. Being responsible however might never be attainable till the present situation and that of the future are considered very pivot, and are well managed by the manager of destiny.

When one looks into the need to be adjustable in nature, one might look on the aspect of being able to access information or ideas that might never be truncated or impaired. What I am saying is that, your level of adjustment determines your level of being able to create things that are not exterminable by the circumstances or factors around it, which can be economic, artificial, biological, political, e.t.c, factors. The nature of upgrade and knowledge one is exposed to has a vast input on the appearance or output of a man. What a man knows is so very critical and very necessary on what he offers to the world or can offer. As said earlier, the series of the operational value learnt in a circumstance or the other is quite very important to the nature of the projection and vision. To learn how to create a cleared vision that can create a perfect beginning and continuity, there is need to have the trait of adjustment. This often gives the key to the free entry and exit of the ideas to make up the uniqueness in its performance to grow and to be functional in all manner of the circumstances. However, generating the ideas that are not exterminable or extinct able is very relevant to the issue of being responsible to one's life, to be able to have a separated destiny that can create other destinies around it.

I have discussed on the upgrade as very vital and necessary values that attract adjustment before now, but I just want to reiterate it that, the values around the upgrade are what makes one to take up crucial decisions. Without the elements of adjustment, there might never be element of taken decision that can constitute the upgrade. What I am saying is that, something must have prompted the need to have an upgrade and adjustment, and that might be termed as the personal interest or information. This is very expedient to be noted at the point of consideration of the adjustment to know that the contribution of the willing or self motivated spirit individual is quite needed to have an accomplishment of any gazette or plan to carry out any upgrade of any type.

Changing of value and tactics are the subject to adjustment and getting set to have a full responsibility to one's life. There might never be favourable change till the systematic change is incorporated in the system of the change. Change is a constant thing and either you as a person is wishes to change or not, change will definitely have its way, which means that, nothing is constant, but change. To then have the change of one's choice, there is need to have a systematic approach and tactics that should make the changes to have a direct value to your information and desire. Adjustment makes one to think of the possibilities in the impossibilities as stated before now, but these impossibilities are never attained without the tactics and approaches to make them accomplished. Having a tactic and style that can make things different is very friendly to the achieving at the greater height and being exceptional. Exceptionality separate men from the others, and demonstrate what you have to the world. If at all, your desire is never to let anyone be in the light of what you do, your exceptionality will never keep you secret and unknown. Being exceptional in the tactics and operational values to create a system that can affect the generation in holistic is very relevant at the point sighting the importance of the adjustment to the full utilization of destiny.

What is termed adjustment can be replacement in holistic sometimes. It can make one to leave a certain idea, thought or concept for a particular course. Being determined and fully set to let go of prestigious things might not be over emphasized at the point of looking ahead or trying to attain the stage of adjustment that can yield result. There must be room for outright replacement of thought and personal presence or participation before a complete adjustment is made. The process is what yield to another development of another phase of life that can be better off of the initial experience. The issues that are not worthwhile must be silent or halt for the relevant ones that can lead to the proposed destination or greater testimony of destiny. Destiny not accomplished is a destiny not prepared for. Therefore, in preparation for the creation of destiny, the issues of adjustment is very relevant, and this can lead to the stage of having a total replacement in the entire system of one's life to have the expected responsibility in one's life assumed.

The whole idea around the adjustment is to have a clue on the importance of it while trying to arrive at the destination of having the huge control over one's life. There is no doubt that, adjustment is one of the most significant issues that must be well examined to have a clue and proper orientation on what life is, compares to its responsibility or what being responsible connotes. There might never be a reasonable direction or coordination of the system that leads to the fruitfulness and betterment without the attention to the circumstances that requires change and adjustment, and they must be reacted to in such a way to meet the desire of the circumstance around the whole situation that leads to improvement and paving way for the avenue to have a full control and responsibility to issues of

Chapter Five(5)

<u>NEVER BE ASHAMED OF RECONSTRUCTION</u>

Most of the people are very sensitive and ashamed of starting afresh when things go abnormal. They tend to look around to evaluate what they have done in comparison with others. One might never be too bothered of restarting his ambition severally before they come into manifestation. There are a lot of vision that entail doing them again and again before they can be actualized, whereas, luckily enough, some people venture into them, and they were able to come forth with the testimony at the first trial. Being a failure at the very first attempt or more than series of attempts does not count you a failure if you understand what it means to have a proper provision for a vision to be accomplished. There must be trait that can move the intention ahead without any form of rejection or shame. There is always series of complexity that are attached to the establishment of purpose, and all these must be well thoroughly administered and taken care of before one can see the need to look above being ashamed to climb up accordingly. In as much as the obstacles attributable to events that preempt achievement are more closer to human, there should be a genuine thought that can see far beyond the limitation to be able to form the force that can convert the challenges to greatness and to ignore the shame of any nature at the point of starting over again.

It is possible to conceive the whole lots of irregularities and view that people are looking at you when you are growing. There are surplus of the various events around everyone that might not allow them to see you or to give any meaningful thought to you or your circumstance when you are not lazy enough to allow them to intervene or to see you. Your inability to take care and to take charge of the events around your destiny prompts other individuals to notice your incapacity. Having people discussing about you can even be a greater advantage when you are successful. Counting shame important or significant at the point of ascending to your destination in life means you have no good idea of the essence of what you need to do or doing. Anyone that does not want shame to over rule his intention must be able to adhere to the management of ideas and continuous pressing further to step above all factors that can create inglorious circumstance around what he does.

There are numerous individuals with series of yardsticks to catch up with their desire in life. There is no one without a yardstick, else, there will never be measure of accomplishment or attainment. The yardstick or measure responsible for a cause or action is quite very relevant at the point establishing the authentification of idea. Good to have it, these yardsticks are not synonymous to one another. No wonder the term success is very complex to arrive at. Someone that so many people counted to be a successful entity still looks ahead to make more success visible, while someone that has not even make a step towards what success means also want to be successful. Your gazette in life should be well explainable to you if at all no one can deduce your intention, but the aftermath effect of your dealing and projection must be able to explain itself clearly without any form of interpretation to the world of the worth of its success. There is always need to have no one as gazette to the level of one's functionality, else, there will always be restriction and factors that might be irresolvable at the attempt of making your thought and ideas notable to the world. To be responsible in life, one must be conscious of the full utilization of making all affairs and composition within his reach and in him to be fully hyper functional and well directed and projected toward the attainment of what he has caught up with, other than projecting to accomplish what someone is projecting. As said earlier, there are lots of the shortcomings to the instances of looking into the affairs of becoming like someone else other than being himself.

Thinking of what people have to say should never be the priority of the order of the event of one's life. Sincerely, criticism should have its direct or indirect contribution to the developmental values. What people say sometimes are the sources of the right information to do greater works or to change the dynamics of operation to attain the stage of no limitation. However, thinking ahead of the information that should create a reasonable outcome or assuming that, the feed back will always be reverse of your intention is always a typical hazard that must be critically managed. Most of the champions only believe in what they can do and do them accordingly without minding or too minding of what the world has to say or the insecurity around their motive. They give the very best of themselves to the issues that can take them to places or ahead of the others in an exceptional manner and yet, believe that the result should justify the means. To be exceptional and different among others, there is always the need to understand your mission in life, and being able to discharge the responsibility that leads to the achievement of such action accordingly to be separated and counted distinct in all ramifications. However, what the people might say or have to say should never dictate the tune of the events around one's life to be able to attain the height of total responsibility to the world by being responsible to oneself.

Independence is an act of being self dependable and reliance. There is no way one can think of the necessary reconstruction of plight or decision if he is not independent. When one is self reliance, he takes the full decision of the activities around his destiny. Take for an example, the owner of an organization is directly and indirectly responsible for the activities around the excelling or not of the organization. He decides on what the employees should do, and he can even instruct the business to be closed down for any days. He recruits and sacks the incompetent hands and decides on the series of varieties of decision that can affect the life of the organization. All these are very convenient and could work just because of his independent nature to demonstrate his contents and views. To have a reconstruction when due to the nature of life that one lives, there is every need to be independent to the level of being able to direct his feeling and strength to the solution around his logics to make reality in existence. It gives courage to step into action and to have the rightful option of challenging the activities leading one's philosophy and view. However, to be self dependence is to be set to have the maximum control and decision that lead one's life to his destination, which means, to be reproductive and take full ownership, there must be independence.

Construction and reconstruction many times do not depict failure. There are many initiative and innovation that took more than 40 to 50 years before they are attained. If not to mention the entire projects, the circumstance that lead to the production of bulb can never be omitted, it took the initiator of this idea several years to be able to complete the assignment and the vision he caught up with. Without the mind set to construct and reconstruct your vision when they are not in line with the definition of the stated objective, there might not be total responsibility of life.

Another point that worth to be mentioned is the issue of not being ashamed of starting over and over till a mission is accomplished. Many successes are squashed because they are not restarted or because of the shame that was considered not to have them in place when they are supposed to germinate. There is every need to have a self esteem in the failure that leads to the attempt to be great and to attain a spectacular purpose.

Many fail to understand that the end point of their ambition is quite very pertinent compares with the shame they pass through. When one can not bring out the advantages that are in the end result of purpose ahead of shame, shame dominate failure. When you can see the true picture and nature of what has motivated you to attempt a purpose, it will be very cumbersome for any irrelevant issues around the circumstance to stand as impediment of any nature.

Shame must be converted to celebration in style and success in its futuristic definition. To pick up an option to be in control of one's life, there are many things that are meant to be in consideration and that must be well thoughtful of. Without being able to look into the failure as the stepping stone to success, there might never be the audaciousness to see the need never to be bothered about what people will say or can say till the mission is attained.

Having the mind of forgiveness is quite very relevant to attain the stage of being in total control of the affairs of his or her life. One thing is to be able to forgive others while forgiving yourself is however the most ultimate. Forgiven others is quite very important, but might never be as necessary as forgiven oneself. The act forgiveness is an act that should be cultivated to be in control. Without being able to forgive yourself, you might never be able to do anything meaningful. Forgiveness of oneself is what agrees with your inner mind that, if at all failure is experience, success can be attained. It begins when one needs a certain thing or the other, but could not get it due to some factors. Not having the expectation should not cause him to think that it is not possible to have them. This is the point at which the soul, mental structure and physical nature agree to go further to make a tangible process that can lead to the greater height. Therefore, without the three being in one accord, there might never be any meaningful outcome or accomplishment. They must work in friendly mode to attain the set objectives. To however have someone that can be best positioned or active to have authority in term of responsibility for his life, there must be element of forgiveness which must transcend through both his immediate environment, who he meets with and in his own personal life.

There is a usual saying that, a coward dies before his time. Timidity is the father of not making possibilities that should lead to the way ahead available. Many stars have been wiped off and many talented individuals are far away to make substantial record due to the level of their inability to withstand the pressure that should have led them to a better privilege. To have constructive nature of life, there is always the need to have the courage to live above the impossibilities. These can be ascribed as seen and unseen in nature. To live above shame, there is need to live above the fear of failure. Hence, the need to have full consideration to the nature of mind set that should create the possibilities when there is no clue of having one.

I have only just tried to relate on the need not to be ashamed of constructing and reconstructing as many times as possible to have the full responsibility to one's life if actually, the life is worth to be lived.

Chapter Six(6)

<u>BE REAL TO YOURSELF</u>

One of the major factors to be deliberated on to have better understanding of the elements that are essential to be solely responsible and to be able to have full fledge control on his or her life is being real to oneself. Being able to determine what you have and placing value on it without minding what others have or not is quite very essential to make one to be actually real. Without being real, the total activities that lead to someone actualization will definitely be unauthentic and fake. Living a fake life makes one to consider oneself arrived or successful when he has not even begun a life. There is no way one can live a real life and yet he is living with what he does not want, or doing what he has no influence over. Being real separate a man in the midst of the numerous and gives one identity that can not be covered. It gives one the mind to set a target and looking for all what it cost to achieve such target. It is a direct creation of oneself and making the real content within one's heart to be actualized.

To however be real, there are several things that are meant to be considered and to be well understood to have the completeness on the reality that makes one to be himself, to have all what it takes to be a custodian of his responsibilities and a champion.

There are thousands of the individuals that can not define themselves to the world in their best ability. The question, who are you? Is very relevant to be able to know what exactly one is meant to achieve and to be able to get friendly with the whole lots till they are well nurtured to create the kind of life that should involve the activities that should make a differentiated logic to be better made human of your desire.

Without knowing that no one can take your place or knowing that you are very necessary to be replaced, there might never be any need for you either voluntarily or involuntarily to assume what makes differential provision for creating a real value. There is no one as valued as you, and you were created in your own special way to make a special assignment attained. Things that are left untouched or undone by you might be the things that constitute the greatest challenges to the issues of the world. And things that are not attained by you might never be able to be demonstrated by any other individual till the world ends. You have a special trait in you, and that special trait should be able to make you to be well outstanding and comprehensively important in your own capacity. However, knowing that you are specially created for an assignment and for the intention that should change the world for the best is one of the most crucial things that should be well understood to be very sensitive to being responsive to the action that leads to the self responsibility.

Having the passion to be real always and at all times is very necessary to have a head way to being real to oneself. Continuous replication of attitude and disposition, and fate make the world to know what one is set to accomplish or his projection. One must be able to make himself very real pertaining to the things he does and to be able to display that which he has passion to do diligently to fulfill reality of purpose.

When one is himself or herself, he does not act under pretence or false representation. To be real to oneself, there is need to be factual and to be actual in the sense that, he represent himself the way he is constantly and makes the necessary improvement in line with the intention till they are made to be the priority of his ambition.

To be real to oneself and to the world, there is no need to count unnecessary meaning or value to the things you do not have or can not do. But you must be able to create life and different degree of impartational world with the little you possess. Mind you, no one is saying that learning a new trick or knowledge is not essential to life, but the reasoning is this, no one can acquire all the knowledge in life, and with this fact, the little that each one acquires must be judiciously in perfect place, to anchor and to bring out the best in him, and to create a platform to distinct him amidst of the other individuals. Things that are not controllable should never control the affairs of one's life not to be able to represent oneself in a reality standard. Some of the considerations are your complexion, your age, your deficiencies, your qualification, money, connection, environment, e.t.c. these things should never form the basis for the inability to make reality value or live a real life.

Do not be intimidated by the things that are not relevant or intimidate others with what you have. What you have or around you should be what the world should count reasonable meaning to for its conduciveness. As a person, you are never supposed to create a platform of intimidation in any way to anyone. Making the world to be part of your attainment is making the world to be friendly with your whole lots of ideas that can make a meaningful contribution in the whole essence. Being intimidated or intimidating others with what you have however might never yield any responsible interest in line with the reality of purpose and being real to oneself. The fear of all sorts must be well dealt with to formulate the basis for the reality of the existence and purpose that should segregate one from the conglomeration of the world populace.

To be out-rightly real, you must be able to have full access to yourself and your total being. If no one could see your fault or see your mistakes, you can see them often at the point of reflection. Try to study them, make the necessary amendment and look for the enlargement. No one is above mistakes, one must be able to check through his or her life once in a while to be able to know where he has gone wrong and to have a replacement or amendment when due to prevent such circumstances in the years to come.

Before one can be real to himself, he needs to understand that no one can give the very best definition of him or interpretation to his value or vision other than him. One must be responsible for himself to give adequate definition of himself, interpret his value or vision and try to demonstrate them accordingly. The set of individuals that are waiting for the other set of individuals to define or interpret them are such that are strictly not independent enough to bring out the values that are hidden in them. There is no thought or decision that has no value of its own, but the ineffective ones can never be of any magnitude or importance. One must be self driving to create the activities around his ambition and to make the very use of his internal composed ability to come forth with the uniqueness that can lead one ahead. To then have the reality of oneself, there must be understanding of the best definition and value that can be extracted right from within a human.

No matter what in life, one can never be changed to another person. Having the mind that you need to be like another person might not realistically make the best out you. There are some special configurations in each man, such that, if your intention is to be like him, a time will come that such configuration that makes him to react or behalf in such a way might be a hindrance to the upper level of one's performance. There must be urged to be yourself constantly, because without being yourself, you might end up becoming no one. And sincerely, there is special feature that should have made the specialty to be in work in the life of everyone. It is a must for all never to consider oneself to be translated to another person or to have a replica of what he has done in such a way he has done it to be living soul that can demonstrate at the peak of the order of the relevance to the existence.

Being real to oneself means being able to have a sensitive position to the things around him. The set of the issues and undertakings must be well studied and handled in such a way to make other valuable experiences noted and experimented. Being conscious of the things around one is an act of having a thorough view on those things, and being able to come forth with the real idea that are connected to the creativity and the whole lots of information that should take the world to the next level. Sensitivity is however one of the major necessary issue that must be well examined to have the real men in existence, and to make out the real self in the context of the responsibility to one's life.

Rationality and thoughtfulness are in line with the series of the option that lead to being real in life. Someone that thinks of being real must be very rational to know the decisions that are worth taking and the ones that should be suspended for the others to create a meaningful intention. So also, being thoughtful means, being able to examine if the rational concept is worth to be taken or not before the action is experimented or after the action has taken place. Rationality and thoughtfulness has to do with how composed human nature is and how well managed the composition can be put to use. It has nothing to do with the age, qualification, race, sex, e.t.c. it has to do with the things that can be seen at the realm at which no one can go with you. They are definitely series of things that are not visible to others, but they are very cleared to the initiator. However, the judgmental decision to take the rightful decision implies the rationality and thoughtfulness. These are very essential at the expense of trying to be real to oneself to have a full control on the life's responsibility.

To be real to yourself and the world in holistic, one must be discussional within and outside. What do I mean by this? I discussed on the issue of being rational and thoughtful before hand, they are the things that have to do with both within and outside. But here, I am concerned on the discussion that takes place within human before they are processed to the final end result of taken decision either within or outside. To be real, one must be very set to see the real values that are contained within him and at the same time, he should be able to reason with the nature of his environment and the people there to create a distinctive outcome that can rightly make him what he should be. Reality of life has to do with both the things that are formed inside and physical, and these two must be well balanced to assume the stage of full reality of one's life, or to define himself appropriately.

To be real to oneself mean that you are not abrogating or assuming yourself to be who you are not. The natures that surround your destiny must be well managed. You must never be too arrogant in any way. While I was still very young, many of my peers believed in borrowing the other friend's vehicle, wrist watches, cloths, e.t.c to the events or to meet with their new female friends. It should not be, one must be able to represent himself the way he is, else he will live a flamboyant life that will make the opportunity that are meant to run in parallel with his destiny elude him. To be your real self, you must be very moderate and humble to present yourself the way you are and how best you can be naturally.

Respect must be decision of one's order to be real. Some people look at how others walk, look, behave, talk, e.t.c to determine if they are respectful or not. Reverse is the case, this depends on how one relate with the others irrespective of his own personal life. What can be seen is not what makes one to be arrogant but what he does at the point of having association with the others. However, to be a real self, there is always the need to be very respectful to be able to accommodate others and at the same time to relate freely with the others to make out a reasonable living. Respect goes with being real to oneself and being able to have the maximum control over his destiny.

All what I have been trying to address are in connection with being real to oneself, and they are very essential to be noted at the point of coming forth with one's personal identification and showing forth his real self to the world.

Chapter Seven (7)

<u>STRUGGLE HARD TO DEFINE YOURSELF</u>

Having self definition is quite very essential to be able to get to the level of self independence and reliance. There is a difference in what people call you and what you call yourself. In the chapter just concluded, I was trying to say that, no one can give the very best definition of you. The only definition that can be given are the ones that you have exhibited to the world. Human nature is composed to the tune of building series of components at their point of desire to move over an issue or the other. To have a distinguished definition, there is always a very difficult time and unpalatable circumstances that are in line with it. Therefore, before thinking of the personal definition, there is need to cross examine the rigor and challenges that are attributable to the foresight to be able to have a full preparation to have a link with what personal definition means and entails.

What is personal definition? This can be said to be an act of giving a brand to oneself. It is an act of making yourself known or real to the world through the set of the elements you possess in you, and directing your total effort to ensure that they are projected in such a manner that they can cause influence in the world as a whole. It has to do with who you are in line with what you have to offer or your disposition. It is one of the most difficult things to assume in life. No wonder, many individuals were unable to discuss the subject matter or have the influence on it till they are extinct or died. There is no way a personal definition can be attained without being confronted with the criticisms and the initial disagreement.

There is no one without something so important to do, and the stages that resolve to the accomplishment of such task is referred to as stages of the self definition. What one goes through in life or undertake while growing or while coming up has a lot of contribution to what he is and his definition. The way things you went through, going through or will go through in life are handled is very pertinent to the best definition you can give to yourself. No man can just stand within a twinkling of an eye to say this is what I am to the world, without creating what he is. The antecedence of the characters that are disclosed or exhibited at the point of growth and engagement are very unique to the definition that one will be accorded.

Therefore, there is need to constantly have the notion of self definition continuously in all the activities that lead to another stage of one's life to have a comprehensive definition of personal worth.

There is always a question to how best one can define himself. Definition of human personality as I said has to do with all what you get involved with. Your intention and direction must be well understood to yourself before you can make it very easy to understand by the people around you. There is no activity of any kind that does not create the arena to display oneself and define oneself accordingly. There is need to often tap into the full utilization of the events that are in association to one's life to create a proper definition of who you are. Things that are done but not in a proper manner are the subtraction to the value that a man should be accorded, what you have done in term of your creativity and acquisition can be the best to define you. Your motive to the way of life can define you and your approaches to the circumstances around you can not be exempted out all that makes your complete definition.

There are numerous things that are meant to be defined in life, such are the way you relate with the people and handle things that has to do with them.

You must be very conscious of how others are treated and also, how their issues are resolved to be able to have an adequate definition. Do not forget, irrespective of what your worth is or your position in life, there will always be change at when due. You can be the best teacher now, but the best of the teachers that will set you parking is on the way, you can be the best orator now, the best is yet to be born, you can be the best of the best in any field now, but the best of the best is yet to be born. So, being relatively considering the others to move ahead is very important while you are advantaged because these set of the individuals might be very relevant while you are coming down.

Some ask questions of where one defines himself. The point is that the world is large enough to experiment your content and philosophy. You may not need to get into the heaven before your definition is given. Things that have to do with the reality of life define themselves while one lives, but they are alive when one does not exist anymore. The series of the activities in the world are large and extremely vast to define everyone if all are attentive to the issues that lead to individual definition. You might not necessarily need to do mighty things before you are defined according to who you are, but having ordinarily things displayed or acted on as if they are extra ordinarily things or making reasonable thought and action in an uncommon way might lead to the definition of personal worth. Therefore, what others might have counted to be a negation or challenges should be made to be the series of activities that preempt one's successful conclusion.

To define oneself means to put oneself in the midst of trial and tribulation. There are many leaders that though they were well defined, but they could not witness the end of their respective definition. There is no way one can define himself without having the relative issues with some individuals, and sincerely, if too much of consideration and focus is not given, it might amount to an abandon purpose in the sense that, the distraction or condemnation in line with it might constitute an end to it. Most of the religious leaders were affected, they struggle hard to make the definition of who they are, many were killed at the point of trying to illustrate their worth and personality, and this is what the definition can cause to humanity. On the other hand, the inventor of different kinds of technological innovation and ideas also suffered the same attribute at the point of making the world to be in the light of their decision to ease the world. Many of these inventors could not achieve anything for more than 40 years, but the set of those ones that could sustain the pressure were made to be fortunate and have record on the amelioration of the discomfort of the existence. Many of them were mocked to their faces and ridicule to the level of ordinarily having the second thought not to continue, but amidst the odds and pains, the respecter and the lover of the dignity in labour created avenue for the rightful outcome and celebration. One must be able and set to give the very best of oneself and all he contains in him to make the personal definition comes into reality. There is different between what someone is and that which another man is, but the difference can not be expressed without the express or implied commitment of the one that should be defined. A man can make series of definition to himself through what he does. No one can give any definition to anyone without what he has done, is doing or going to do. This is the reason why one must on constant basis make a proper contribution and ideas that should give the best of definition.

Demonstration of the definition travels far than just saying it. To have a definition that travels far or to be able to persuade thousands of the people that you do not know or might never meet with in life, there is utmost need to be a demonstrator of what you define.

If love is your focus, then, the appropriate demonstration of affection and love should be seen in you. If you are a leader, your acts should reveal it to the people around you, unlike the self imposed leaders of most of the African nations. If you are a freedom fighter, you should be constantly involved in making the school of thought felt in the midst of the people, you must never be the one cheating or defrauding others. To be a scholar, there must be elements that portraits you to be a scholar, not just by your saying or what you have acquired that many could have achieved if they are privileged. Definition has to do with the nature of legacy that one creates for the future. It has to do with those things that term one to be humane or not. It has to do with your attitude and action towards diversified nature of issues, and it has to do with you and you all alone with your total relationship with the world.

There is always the need to be a bit rugged in thinking and action. I keep on saying ruggedness is part of life. I do not mean that one should be a tout or area boy, but what I am saying is that, life is not friendly to anyone, but when one can stand on his feet to defend what he wants out of life, life becomes amiable to such individual. Nothing comes freely without pain or difficulties, but the difficulties and pains that are visible are not what should term a man a failure. There must be possession of the mind that can live above the impossibilities and all sorts of the impositions by the nature. However, before one can be availed the privilege or the right of the order, there is need to be rugged or resilience in nature. When things are tough, the goal getters discover their possibilities to convert activities around them to their benefits, whereas, the failure could only see the difficulties and impossibilities.

However, to be rugged in nature is very essential as stipulated before now, but there is always the need to be teachable. At the point of expressing oneself in term of personal definition, there is very great need to be sensitive to the mistakes around. Despite the rugged mind, there must be control and orderliness in the exhibition of intention. Truly, there are a lot of things that one might not condole while trying to make a personal illustration of one's definition, but to learn more sometimes, there is always the need to be attentive and reason with what others do or say. These acts should form the basis of the best reaction that should define one in the midst of their tribulations and castigation. Be hard, but be very soft to the changes on the wrong acts to amend them.

In the subject before now, we deliberated on the vital reason for one to be directly or indirectly involved in the act that leads to personal definition. I just want to quickly say again that, it is very necessary for the world to define you based on what they have seen. Though, they could have formed their basis on the relative ideas they can access, but one must be able to undertake series of the operations that are notable and recordable to champion or live above their hypothesis. There is no crime in the definition given by the world, but it will never be meaningful to have a wrong definition and at the same time, record reveals same definition as it was expressed. However, the need to have the full urge to take the direction of what makes the final basis of the definition that makes a man. You can give very different definition of yourself irrespective of what the world had defined you to your suit when you have the mind to differentiate yourself, and to make what your worth to be well understood to the generation.

Your final outcome of your disposition should genuinely mention your real person and paint you the very right representation or recognition. Being actively involved in the series of the things that are very closely related to your objective and vision while living make the direct perfect analysis of your being without anyone having the influence on it. What a man might not see by himself are best illustrated by the things he has gone through or doing. It might be very complex for one to see all about himself, but it is very quite easy to be accessed by the people who are observant of what you do or who take cognizance of its effects on the environment you live, and its contribution to both humanity and societal values. If that is the case, there is always the need to make a decision that can lead to a better fortune or define oneself to the best suitable standard for the sake of the reputation and cause of the rightful pedigree to make a meaningful end result that can guarantee a solid constructive decision to mention you accordingly while you live or to be mentioned when you are no more.

The necessary steps are however very necessary to follow or to adherent to in order to be able to have a full perfect definition that is worth while to command the authority or control over the unrealistic nature of the information or rumors that were made or created before the time of your performance and exhibition of your personal definition.

Chapter Eight (8)

HONESTY AND STRAIGHTFORWARDNESS

To be straightforward means to be easy and uncomplicated in nature. It means that trait to demonstrate what you have to offer. It means a life that is not separated from what he says or narrated. It can be termed to be a person that can be relied on and can be depended in his absinthial, who can be predicted on his developmental ideology or things that has to do with the increase and advancement.

When one lives a basic life amidst the people, he is often termed as a straightforward minded individual. It can be an attribute that is very consistent and ever fruitful when it is dissect or critically examined. It can be said to be a situation where one is not moved or hindered to be justified at the course of making decision that could move his intention ahead in midst of the obscurity and instance of the negative agitation that might be willing to truncate the whole essence of the good intention.

This is often arrived at by having synergetic performance between honesty and transparency. It is noted when one understand better of the right things or decision to take, and he is always ready to stand for the decision to manifest without minding the frustrating efforts around its experimentation.

To however be able to live a meritorious life and to be in control of one's life, it is very essential for one to be mentally configured with the things that are subjected to the developmental intention and increase at all times to be able to demonstrate values that are impartational and quite important to the advancement of the world.

Sincerely, when one is straightforward, there are more than enough benefits that are always very closely related with his living. To mention few; rest of mind; when one is straightforward and very honest, he has the opportunity of having rest of mind. He is often not afraid of anything or thinking irrelevantly to have either a consideration on what people say or what they might say. The right minded people are always very blunt and direct in their thinking and very comfortable as a result of their contribution. Therefore, to have a rest of mind, there is always the need to be honest and straightforward.

Another important aspect worth mentioning is the issue of having a straight thinking. If one is not honest and straightforward in his aspect of his life, he might find it very complex to have straight thinking. Without a cleared vision and consideration, there might never be straight thinking. The position of your mind has a greater value on what you can access at the realm unknown, and it has a great magnitude of the things you can produce internally. To however be able to attain the instance of being responsible for one's life, there is extreme need to be able to be very honest and straightforward to have straight thinking that can generate the undiluted and unpolluted information that can constitute change and transformation.

Being honest and straightforward generates trust and dependability amidst of the people. If your passion is to be in control of your life and to be responsible, there is always the necessity to have all it takes to build trust and higher level of dependability to the other individuals around you. It is very easy to think of trust and dependability, but it is hard earn, because it can never be actualized without your full participation and creating such an avenue that can translate to it. Mostly, in the developing region or areas, we often fight to have it or to be decorated with trust and dependability, forgetting that it is self created and demonstrated. Your demeanor and conduct at the point of exhibiting your values and relating with the world in holistic prompts your expectation and reward on the trust and dependability.

Very vital enough to be mentioned again is the ability to travel far. To be able to travel far does not mean that you are moving physically, but it means the ability to move without being moved. This means that, you are somewhere and you are everywhere without your too much of effort than what you have done as a result of being honest and straightforward. To be frank, one of the most basic transmitter of the good reputation and good handiwork is either the good news or the bad ones created by the populace within the environment of their living and in fact, sometimes outside their immediate living. To however travel far, you must be able to summit to the decision to have the worth of personality that the propaganda can not destabilize or frustrate. You must be well groomed to the level of having the full result in the midst of the abnormality, and allow the pressure around your objection never to exterminate your right decision. Things done that you might never have the privilege to administer at a point or the other are termed the structure of the activities that moves you farther in repute and definition. You must be able to create instance that can translate you to higher level or places you might not be able to cover by yourself with the attribute of honesty and straightforwardness, and these amount to what make you responsible for your life.

Increase in value is a point that most people fail to consider while looking into the issue of life. There might not be an alternative to the increase of value and being well groomed without being honest and straightforward. Living a perfected life and thinking of the possibilities, and ensuring the possibilities become an act that will exist to live above all nature of impediments that might be willing to squash it is very relevant to assume increase in the value and reasoning. To then identify the importance of the honesty and straightforwardness, the total expedient value will be centered on the life's responsibility.

There are many of the individuals that are never having anything substantial to secure themselves in the time of creation of relative issues that are meant to impede their destiny. This is how life works, when you aim at a higher level, there will always be many distraction to ridicule or derail you from the intention. Propaganda of no basis and those with the basis will be outlined to make sure the intention is not accomplished. But if you have a genuine act and past, and you were very honest and straightforward at the point of discharging the obligation in connection with your reason while the time was being spent, there will always be the courage to have a defensive confidence and refer to them at when due if there is any need to have them mentioned.

Boldness is another very meaningful ingredient that can be extracted out of being honest and straightforward. I just concluded on the aspect of having evidence for defensive purpose in the just concluded discussion. When there are various set of the defensive products to attest to the ill talk and the propaganda around one's destiny, there will be every tendency of having the courage to be outstanding and to defend personal worth accordingly. Boldness is a thing of the mind, and it has to do with what you have within. If what you have within is not enough to keep you moving, there will be disconnection between what you have and that which you can attain. And when what you have is not commensurate with what you need to actualize them, then, there might be fear or panic along the line on the defending or attaining a specific motive that your view is in connection with. Being bold is as a result of being honest with yourself and being able to inspire oneself from the within to be mentally and physically prepared for a certain bargain or contest that must be won. Therefore, if there is no room for boldness, there will never be any means to be set for what it entails to have a full responsibility to one's life.

Being honest and straightforward means being able to persuade the world in the whole essence, most especially when the world has tested and proof your worth to be depended on to act on behalf of them. Without being honest or straightforward, there might never be the attribute of persuasive in one's life. The world wants to test and proof you beyond doubt before they listen to you or have you to be at the helm of control. They want to know how reliable you are to offer you their trust and confidence. Therefore, being able to demonstrate the value of honesty and straightforwardness that are accessible and testable can give a better confidence to the world. However, when the world discovers that you are a man of your word and that you are reliable, they tend to listen to your notion and advise at the point of given them, and they tend to yield to your word of advise and control, believing that you know of what you say and has a foresight that had defined you in the years past, and with the fact that, they are well assured that you will never deny them if at all there is a challenge or the other. Being persuasive is very relevant in the assessment of human worth at the point at which his responsibility towards his life is necessitated.

Being a leader is not made in a day. A leadership obligation and appointment is often created gradually and systematically in line with the series of the activities that are attached with the lineage of one's disposition and character. To be a leader, there is always the need to have the attributes that were mentioned before now. A leader might not force himself on the other individuals before becoming one. Most of the leaders assume the state and stage of leadership just because of what they have done, doing or what people perceived that they can do through the assessment of their past worth and justification. Honesty and straightforwardness are very essential to have completeness in the attribute that create leadership or assume human to be appointed as leaders. Therefore, it is quite very pivot to know that, one must be able to lead himself first before he can lead others, and by so doing, he must work earnestly to possess the attributes that are relatively crucial to be able to be a leader, which however becomes the attribute to be responsible in all ways to attain the full impetus of living a responsible life.

Your must be involved in the activities at all times, you must make sure that your presence is constantly felt and well represented. Creating activities around you or your vision must be very necessary. Where there is no opportunity should be an avenue for the best of your advantages. Without having a function or the other, there might never be a means to have any legacy fulfilled. Without looking out for the best to be achieved, there might not be any urge to do beyond normalcy and to be exceptionally positioned. Activities not created can never be assessed or proven, and the assessment that can make a man to be lured to the ways the activities are resolved can not be completed. Therefore, to be very inclusive and well recorded for the height of recognition that can add value to the personal worth or recognition of one's pedigree to have a full responsibility on one's life, there is need to have the creation of activities that can prove the real worth of a man in his composition.

To be tested on the honesty and straightforwardness, there must be option of having increase in the number of friends or being friendly to the point of being able to be evaluated. Sincerely, not having the apex height of friendliness might not disadvantaged you from being assessed, but the reality point should be made noted that, when one is friendly, he can always be very prone to what can lead to the justification of his appropriateness or integrity. Therefore, there is no way someone can be very responsible in any form without being ready to be associated with his environment. This however creates the platform that defines your character and the level of honesty and straightforwardness that determines your genuineness to the world.

Being honest means that one is open minded and simple hearted to receive and treat information accordingly. Without a mind that can absorb information and its contents, there might never be the grace and the tendency of being able to manufacture the products therein. Honesty and straightforwardness means being open minded and maximally simple in logics and its applications. It promotes the relationship standard of the friendliness and introduces people to your nature of living which can be very beneficial to your future glory or expectation. The sets of the individuals that are open minded are often tenable to the uncommon ideas that can move the world to the stage of great imagination and fulfillment. They are always very reasonable to convert decision to values and make out what other men can not see to be what they can introduce to their lives to have a better living. Having an open mind is then necessary to someone who aspires to be responsible in term of his control over his life and destiny.

One might be cautious, but you might never try to doubt what other individuals can do. To have the due trust from the men around you, there is extreme need to have the trust in them. it is noticed that, many fraudsters and gangsters are inclusive in the world economic function now, but yet, we still have the set of the individuals that are very reliable, you must never be someone that hand picks your friends, but must be able to understand how to relate with every other individuals irrespective of their tribes, position, sex, level of education, religion, belief, e.t.c. To be termed to be an honest or straightforward man, you must be very direct and have a relationship undiluted with the people around you and in the world in holistic. However, being cautious is not a sin or a barrier to your level of being represented or identified, but an avenue to be availed the instance of knowing who you are by the general world.

Another thing that is worth to be mentioned is the issue of being attentive to the minor works or obligations that one undertakes. Those things that one might not consider to be anything while undertaking them sometimes are quite very expedient to be noted, and they can sometimes be the best avenue of evaluating a man. What I am saying is that, there is no work that is not important and there is no obligation that can not define your personality or give your actual meaning, if that then is the case, there is extreme need to fix yourself into the resources that can help out to know how best your attribute can be manifested. This aspect is as well very expedient when one looks into the area of honesty and dependability to attain the height of having a full responsibility that should make a man.

Having respect for the others can not be over emphasized. There is need to bestow due respect to others while being involved in an activity or the other. One of the most crucial thing that must be attended to as a rational human being is the ability to accord the due respect to the others irrespective of their age and position. Without a good relationship that was mentioned before hand, there might not be room for being respectful. Also, without knowing there is none that is not important and relevant in his own way, one might not understand the logics to be respectful. Being the boss or the initiator of the business does not mean that you should not give the due respect when expected, and being the least in the organization does not prevent you from doing so. The interest of the others must be put into the consideration always to be able to understand what it is to be respectful and to gain the honour to the absolute honesty and straightforwardness. Giving respect to the others can never be absent at the expense of looking out for the due responsibility that leads to issues of life.

Chapter Nine(9)

<u>SELF DISCIPLINE</u>

In this very chapter, I will not talk at length, but I will only elucidate what it takes to be self disciplined. There are a lot of elements that are amalgamated to determine self discipline, and these sets of the items will be listed and briefly examined.

Self control- this is an ability to have the direct and indirect influence on what one does. Being able to say no to some certain things in life, such as, eating habit, stealing, working, sleeping, talking, wasting time on the irrelevant things, adding value educationally and vocationally, e.t.c. A man should be able to control himself in term of the activities of his or her involvement to have a successful ending. Time that is not control might be emptied in nature or unyielding.

Patience- you might not need to attend to all things around you. There are some things that one should look at as if they have not happened. There must be the mind that tolerates others on their wrong doing and inability to maturely behave themselves. Everyone is prone to reacting to the issues most especially when they are not such that they expect or such effect that is not too reasonably. There should be an overlook of some event that leads to other. There are so many things that are happening for you to gain full insight in the situation around you, and if one is not too attentive, the logics might never be extracted. Therefore, one of the attributes of the self discipline is to be able to have the due patient to tolerate others. This then, amounts to the height at which one can operate as human which speaks directly or indirectly on his level of being responsible as human.

Be direct and factual- being the fact that you are patient does not mean that you are not direct or being factual in your ideology and doings. You must allow the people to know where you are heading to. You must be able to defend your statement and doings at all times without being afraid of anyone. Your statement must never be uttered by the decision around it. Standing on the fence might not help your personality, but being able to determine where you are and projecting towards it. A direct minded makes the world to know his direction and try his possible means to allow the world to understand the essence of making it real. Direct and factual men are never under estimated at the point of making men that are responsible for their lives, and this can not be exonerated from the issues that must be visited while checking on what self help means.

Seeing the need to deliver- there is different between you and what you can see to achieve. There must at all times be creation of the uniformity of who you are and what you can see. When what one can see is not what one does, it implies creating a dream that is not needed to make a meaningful impact and to affect the decision around you. The fact that the decision is made to execute something should gratifies the need and urge to seeing that they are delivered. There are numerous of the thousands of the ideas and worth of the men that are meant to have added to the ordinary way of life, but they are not composed and structured in a way they can execute their desire. The difference between who you are and your intention is simply what you can do or can not do, there is always the need to be well involved and prepared for the action that follows your intention to have the same outcome coming out of your action. This implies your level of operation to be involved in what makes your decision and personal worth equivalent with themselves. The attempt to balance the ratio of operation between what you say and do is very important while looking into the basis for being self disciplined and examining what it takes to be responsible.

Timeliness – timeliness is a very crucial aspect of life that should be well cross examined to be able to conclude on the standard of the self discipline that should depict the responsibility of a man. Timeliness is a frame work that leads to the execution of an assignment. There are thousands of the things that are very relevant only when they are made to be actualized when they are needed. Meeting with the decision of time and the need of time is quite very expedient to make a meaningful effect and to be productive accordingly. There is always the need to make oneself very active and responsive to the height of being able to act at the moment of request and importance. There is always time for everything in life, and the time duration and placement must be observed to have a completion or due reasonable outcome. So, there is no way one can be disciplined without being timely in nature. He must be represented and involved when due without any delay or set back to be late or being unable to accomplish accordingly.

Cautiousness-the act of cautiousness means being able to be careful and sensitive to the things around one. There are several thousands of the things that are relevant in life, but they can never be seen or noticed or accessed when the carefulness in not of concern.

One can only react on the things he can view or extract from what he has access to or living with him. Being cautious means the act to be involved in the activities that are created to resolve the imbalances in the world, and those who should set a man up for his purpose. It can as well be said to be carefulness on one's thought and action. Being mindful of the imperative outcome of the decision that should be valuable to the existence and looking at creating an enviable contribution that is set as legacy to the developmental issues in life means cautiousness. This is an attribute that is as well worth to be considered while looking at the area of the life's responsibility.

Respectfulness- self discipline entails a lot of attributes. Being respectful means the attitude of being able to stream line one's action or inaction or consider others quite very important and worth to be honoured at the point of doing any thing that got to do with the activities around the issues of life. Most culture consider age and other criteria very essential to accord people their respect, but ordinarily, respecting oneself is quite very relevant and compulsory not to mention of respecting the others. There is a saying that, respect is reciprocal, this means that the amount of respect to the others result to that which will be accorded to you. Treating other with respect is very important and greatly necessary to have respect from the others in the world. However, to be self disciplined and to fulfill the kind of respect that is essential to the issue of responsibility and being in full control, there is need to observe the things that bring about respect.

Fruitfulness- fruitfulness is just the ability to bear fruits. I discussed the issue of being passionate to deliver promptly before hand. Fruitfulness means the act of directing attention and strength towards things that can generate result. One must be result oriented to be made accordingly. What one does without the full expectation of result might be action that leads to no where or that has no basis for its occurrence. Living without any concrete issues around your life to attain might be termed ordinary and waste. Take for an example, no matter how good a football team is, without the end result which is to score on the football pitch, there might not be any relevance to their activeness. Therefore, the discipline minded is always very considerate of the end result or outcome of their action. However, this is very unique to the issue around the responsibility for one's life.

Being energetic- means creating the internal strength that can withstand the pressure around the objective one positions his mind towards. Before one can achieve anything in real life situation, there is always to perceive the demanding factors and necessities to be able to have the full preparedness to accomplish such task. Being energetic might not mean being strengthened physically all alone, but it cut across being strengthened in the mind to carry out an objective. The internal factors should be able to control the physical factors till they are accomplished. Even when an assignment can not ordinarily be accomplish by one, he can be convinced of having the best outcome in it through the use of the other relative outlets and avenues. To be self disciplined, the issue of energetic must be chief of consideration and worth to be mentioned, this however forms the basis for the representation and the fulfillment of purpose that must lead to responsibility.

Dependability- I will not talk much on the issue of dependability any longer. Insights were already given to the scenario surrounding its meaning earlier on. But to be self disciplined, there is always the need to have all it entails to be reliable and dependable. The dependable men are the most outstanding men that the world follows. To however command the respect or to have the basis for having the maximal control on your life's issues, there is always the need to take into the full consideration the issues of dependability.

Controllability- most of the leaders have lost their battle as a result of their inability to entertain the decision and clues that should have made them exceptional in their discretional act. No matter how difficult you are or one can be, there will definitely be set of individuals that are always sharing their thought with him. These set of the individuals are not with you by mistake. They are there for you to learn one or two things from them. They can be the very first option to receive a feed back if you are so real in your attitude to the issue of life. I have not said that one should implement what they say even when they are wrong, but I can say it courageously that, out of all information that can be received, there will always be element of construction in them. The vital nutrient that is responsible for the increase and developmental intention are very quite needed for the formation of better ideology and activities around it. Two heads are better than a single one as they say not to talk of the multiple heads working for a purpose. There is always the essential need to have other opinion relevant to what you do since no one is an island of knowledge. A disciplined mind considers the others first before him and tries as much as possible to know better of their needs to excel. Therefore, to gain control to the path that leads to exceptionality and discovery of new insight and being responsible for the issues of life, there is always the request for one to be self disciplined.

Rationality- there are some issues that are self judgmental. You may not need anyone to tell you that they are wrong or right. There are some decisions that one makes to favour himself without the due consideration of the others but the mind and innate man keeps on reminding one of its unjustifiable position. Intuition in every man and the innate set up are very active at the point of doing wrong, but most men ignore their conscience and the warning signal. One of the most decaying natures of the irrationality is the issue of the self centeredness and greed, and these must be separated from the human nature to conquer the inadequacies that surround the world developmental agenda. To be rational means to be right thinking and to be able to be selective out of the numerous decisions to have the best option that can lead to the world enlargement at all cost. Rational development can only be evidence of the rational thought and constructive pattern of life. To then arrive at the stage of having the responsibility towards one's life, there is a must to be rational and not that all alone, but to set the paste to the highest level of rationality.

Constructiveness- this is another important element that must be considered at the point of creating an indefatigable structure to make the self discipline realistic and of greater importance. There is never any action that is not constructive that can hold, there is no action or activities without a solid basis that can lead to any meaningful outcome. Having a structure is very essential to having a result that can be materialistic and create result accordingly. Self disciplined minded are always with the structure that can extend to another activity. They are always connected with the values that can make difference and peculiarity. The architectural pattern of any attempt is quite very relevant to know how relevant and viable such attempt can be. However, a self disciplined minded must have what it entails to have a good structure that can compete with the circumstances around it, and live meritorious evergreen nature of life. Constructiveness however covers the path of the living that makes a good responsibility to be in charge of one's life.

Smartness- being smart means being tidy and neat. It can as well be said to be an act of being able to key into an action voluntarily at when due. It can be an act of being clever and intellectually configured to carry out an assignment. It means thinking ahead of the circumstance that necessitates an activity of personal involvement to have an ease paste to resolve the issues within the contents around it. Smartness is one of the necessary elements that depict the level of one self level of disciplined. And to be sincere, this has its enormous contribution towards how best one can perform in the area of the life's issues.

Being guided and gauged- there must be limit to all things in life. Life without limit and gauge is a life that might not be able to come forth with any meaningful result. There is need to have limit to all series of involvement of the human endeavors. When one cross examines enjoyment, it is often very comfortable and interesting compares with being involved in the other area of the economic functions. Frankly, life can not be only rested on the fun of it all alone else, there will not be life or living in futility. There must be check and balance in what one does to be able to attain the height of glory and to surpass ordinary. Making limits to the issues of life is very expedient to be able to have a conclusive result else the expected benefits might still turn to an adverse effect on one's path. To be self disciplined, one must be self regulated and adherent to the system that should be observed to take control of the activities that create opportunities around you. Without being guided and gauged, there will be massive wastage of effort and ideas which might never allow the very best of the intention to be effectively germinated or erected. You must be able to know when you are meant to move in to start a particular activity, you must know when you are supposed to stop or discontinue else, there will be reversal of its expectation if control is not in place. Every one wants to be known and to have something meaningful contributed to the world in which they live, but not everyone are contributory to what makes their effort visible or attained. Time is one of the most essential attributes to the greatness and making decision that are developmental in nature. But when the timing or the time management is not well managed, it results to the dead end of the option or decision. There must be limit set for different activities that human gets engaged with, most especially the ones that got to do with the fun and social aspect of life to be able to have something substantial and worthwhile accomplished. Without being able to control oneself there might not be what is termed as self disciplined and having an end result of being in charge of one's destiny.

Being developmental- to be developmental means having the mind set to constantly see the need to be available for the development and increase in the world. It means seeing the importance in the contribution that one has to offer while he lives. Thinking that has do with how the imbalances in the world can be ameliorated and adjusted. This is looking for the best ways at which value and traits can be converted to experiences that pave way for the solution. It is quite very imperative and extremely required of human to be developmental, to affect his environment continuously rationally in the things that are assembled in the nature of living. The issues of the world are centered on the inactiveness of the human nature to at all cost invest their time on the things that are available in them. There is extreme need to be functional in the capacity of making a meaningful inclusion in the system around us to be developmental. So pathetic that many individuals with the developmental nature of the component are often preferred their inclusion in the destructive activities instead. To be self disciplined and to have what is yours in your care, there is always the need to be very inclusive and developmental. A developmental mind can access more of the opportunities that can not easily be seen by the others.

To quickly round the sub topic self discipline up, I will like to say that being self controlled and disciplines is very relevant to have a head way over the others and to shape one's life to his taste in the event of living.

There is no one that can not manage himself, but not all of us can control ourselves. The difference between self discipline minded and some one that has no control over his life is that, one can plan and yield to the plan, while the later can plan or might not be able to plan and, or not able to implement their planning or objectives. Therefore, it is very pivot for everyone to know that he can make the futuristic events attainable when he can be disciplined to take the necessary steps at when due.

Chapter Ten (10)

<u>MARKET YOURSELF, PRODUCTS AND SERVICES</u>

Marketing is an act that is demonstrable and very real in practice. There are many things that are of greater value but yet, they are not known or noticed because of the place they are found or located. When you can not move into the operation that leads to the marketing in life, one has not begun the action that leads to the end destination. The technological improvement has however added to the value of marketing without being too much stressed up. What do I mean, it is very possible for marketing to take place from your hidden place without any too much of effort for the entire world to know about your intention. There are diverse ways to experiment marketing at the present age compares with the old nature of the marketing strategy. One of these ways can be seen in the use of social media, advert placement on the air, posters, inclusive of the old nature of hawking, e.t.c. I am only trying to say that, to have a control over destiny or on one's life, there is always the need to be involved in the activities that must make those qualities, services and products to be known to the world. Take for an example, if you are the best shoe cobbler, without the action that leads the shoe to the world to have access to the series of the products, there might not be too much of the customers coming around to have them. The information might only be refrained to the set of the individuals that are given the opportunity to have direct assessment on the shoe by seeing them and also, those who are privileged to see the shoe on the legs of the people who bought them can as well be persuaded. The restraints and refrain to the number of the individuals that are available to the information that leads to the services and products available are very essential when one is looking at the economic of scale of a business. The viability of the business is rested on the number of the transactions and activities that are undertaken in such business. Therefore, there is every need to be engaged in the work of the marketing to make whatever you do well known and available for the use and consumption. This particular aspect is not studying the commodities all alone, but it is also checking through the services and personal inclusion. Therefore, any of the involvement that one gets involved with must be made well publicized for their awareness and general public usage. The best canteen and restaurant or rostrum are somehow found in the hidden places, very hard to believe, but when you move into the jungle, you will definitely find better palatable and sweet soup dished out for consumption. The essence of the passage and this particular heading is rested on the need to be involved in the series of the activities that make the vision to be worthwhile. Marketing is very expensive and worth taken to be integrated into the system that creates a better nature of the activities that lead to greater luck and fortunes.

What is market? A market is not referred to a specific place. It can be the avenue to communicate with the others with the variety of the techniques that were mentioned before hand on the essence of a cause of an action, product or services. A market is termed to be the place at which the intention of both the seller or producers and the consumers meets before decision are taken by the consumers on either accepting them or not. It can be defined as an action or place that gratifies the movement of ideas, notion, services or commodities of different nature for the end users to make their selection on the relative choices of the desire and with a good grade. One can refer to it to be a place where sellers and the buyers meet to transact or an agreement that brings both buyer and seller together to transact. The availability of the chance or opportunity to transmit information or to get engaged with the buyers and the world at large can be referred to a market.

Marketing is relevant to be able to make the vision, services and commodity well known and identified to the world. Without being able to have the direct access to the information that leads the intention of the buyers to pick up or have the desire to pick up the products, there is no marketing. There are thousands of the services, products and commodities that one picks up not as a result of its immediate need, but because of the urge for it or the access he has to pick them up. Sincerely, without marketing, there might never be such grace being availed to the populace. Marketing makes the world to have access to the series of the information about things and sometimes stands as persuasive elements that inform the buyers the need to consume the materials under discussion. Marketing makes the world to have information on the diverse kind of products, services, ideas, e.t.c. and for them to have the comparison with the others to be able to make a worthwhile decision. It leads to competition among the sellers, service providers and producers. When what you do have closely competitive products or better ones than what you do, and the populace is in the light of the difference, there is always the probability of changing over to better ones or buying the ones that are more qualitative and reliable. Marketing leads to creating all measures to have improvement on the nature of the kind of the activities one is involved with before hand. When one discovers that what he does is not as valuable or worth compares with the every other commodities or services in the global market, it forces the production and service to be more effective in term of adding value at all cost to be exceptional and to be worth noted. Either directly or indirectly, it gives more effort to the economic function and activities because more of the creativity knowledge is given the grace to display and to increase their possibility to gain full control of the market. There are thousands of the functions and the essence of the market that can be mentioned, but the intention is not rested on this particular assignment, hence, there will be need to move ahead in the context of being responsible for one's life.

However, it will not be too smart not to quickly examine how one can market himself. I have said a lot about the numerous means and avenue of marketing products and services, but there are some things that are very vital to be understood as regards the reasons that lead to effective marketing or best way to market. The issue of branding can not be excluded or underestimated at the point of cross examining the issue at hand. Branding is an act of being well represented with the product and services that are inclusively the right of the seller, producer and service provider. To say brand means, creating an identity for a specific intention that makes such consumable items to be very easily recognized and determined. This can be said to be the definition, caption, name, logo or signage that means the holistic representation of your services or products. It is said to be the nature of the separation that segregates a product from the others even when the owners are not represented or presented. It is said to be the reputation of an organization, of product, services or provider so distinguished. Branding is very important to move the market or to be a top market decision maker. This can certainly be a means to market products, services and personal definition.

Making of the qualitative services and production is simply another measure to have a resounding marketing. When the natures of your provisions are quite more qualitative in nature, the populace tends to react to having such provision without much of effort. The products and services speak for themselves, and move the market without much of the effort of the owner. Qualitative and durable products and services are often better economically, and are more encouraged in the market environment. The prices of the product also have a greater decision on how best the attention can be given to them. If the products or services are worth to be taken but they are not reasonable in prices, the consumers might not find them too necessary to pick them up. Also, if the gaps on the prices of such consumable items are wider than necessary than the others, there might never be a positive reaction to them also. I meant that, there must be reasonability on the intention of fixing prices not to send the customers away from the business idea since there are always an alternative to the consumables. Also, one must strife to make sure that there is constant supply of the commodity and service. Services and commodities are meant to be very close to the arm's length of the consumers. They can only pick up what they can access or can see on constant occasion. Finding makes us to understand that having the products available for consumption when needed might not mean that the products and services are immediately of concern for their consumption, but just for an exhibition that invites or calls the attention the consumers to the consumables to be picked up for their respective time consumption. However, there are different things that are very necessary to be able to create a perfect marketing strategy and to make the services and commodities well known to the world, in the book the need to do a thorough marketing for the full attainment of the organization intention, there will be more time and logics to have better explanation and discussion on the series of issue.

There is always the need to be involved adequately on the marketing techniques and the operation that leads to it. The owner of the business or the initiator of the ideas might never be secluded from being fully involved in the activities that create an enabling environment for such services and consumption to be available at demand and request by the consumers. Therefore, the need for the initiator and the emancipator of the ideas and initiation to be fully engaged therein in the activities that makes the whole scenario working.

One must be very efficient and be well alert to make the competency in him or her to be thoroughly displayed and exhibited to the tune of creating something worthwhile that can make the consumers to have a shift in their concern for the other competitive nature of the other consumable items.

Without being efficient and competent, there might not be an upgrade or improvement that should constitute a better performance in term of productivity and provisions.

Being adjustable in life is very necessary to be able to comply with the development, tactics and strategies that lead to the effectiveness and total improvement during and post production phases. Life is not static, so also every things in it. There will be constant changes to suit the transformation and translation of the world. And as a result of this, there is always the very crucial need to have an adjustable agenda, not only agenda but to be adjustable in nature to have the full control over the relative issues that might be controversial to be resolved.

Being dynamic has to do with one's potency to convert all activities around for himself or for the purpose of creating a developmental agenda to the logics in existence ahead. The words that go with dynamic are being self motivated, active, energetic, vibrant, e.t.c. what I am saying is that, to be able to have the expected result on the issues of the marketing of any kind of the commodities or services, there is always the need to have the attribute of dynamism to attain a full accomplishment.

Being strategically composed is as well very relevant to have an edge way on the marketing aspect of the commodities and services. There must be thorough strategies that can create a profitable end result. Without this, there might not be ability to transfer the commodities and services to the end users which invariably means that, there might not be any need for continuation of such activities or intention.

Being learned and widely exposed is another very important nature of human composition that must be inclined with. The type of the information and exposure one is accessible to have a greater impact on the nature of the end result and how competitive his logics and outcome will definitely be. To access the highest of the order of the nature of service and production, there are a lot of relevant in the nature of your background either educationally or informally. The two axis of life have one or two things to contribute to the level of efficiency and productivity in the projection of idea or set of ideas.

However, these are the sets of the brief ideas to the essence of marketing and how one can market himself to achieve the greater height of proposition and vision in term of services and provision for the production of commodities.

The concern of where do you sell or distribute your product has been from the time immemorial an issue of deliberation. The point remains that, there is none of the activities that are created with a singular motive of affecting the world that is not substantial or crucial, but the major constraint on having the clue on their importance is as a result of not knowing how to get them to the places of their uses. Without being able to discover the actual place at which what you do are needed or required, you might not understand how important you are in the world. Therefore, I can say that, you are as expedient as someone that is well recognized or known today as a result of their ability to understand on time where they are relevant and decided to get themselves inclusive passionately for the people around them to recognize their worth and importance. You are more relevant than someone or those who counted you not, when you are able to allocate your strength to your place of relevance.

However to be relevant at the point of marketing tactics, there is always a matter of necessity to be involved personally. The first marketing in life start from the initiator of the idea or set of the ideas. It is very expedient for one to be well nurtured on having the intuition and logics on the things that are relevant to life and the need for them to be provided. One must be very sincere with the worth and be able to show vast critics before moving such intention to the world. The capability to get one involved and to create a reasonable contents around the usefulness and the criticism can be an assisting provision for a perfect marketing. Looking at where should the market should be sold therefore amount to having oneself inclusive in the list of the consumers that are enclosed to use the products and services. As an owner of the idea or thought, you must be able to see the genuine reason of the use of the material or logics behind your vision. The vision must be very necessary for you and the nature of relevance must be such that it cut across your need. When one fails to do what he has the feeling and passion to do or that has a tremendous contribution to him, he might not be able to gain the full insight on the aspect of its major improvement and concern to upgrade such. The initiator of the ideas are the first set of individuals that are meant to carter for the market of what they do, they must be friendly and constantly using the logics and consumable items to be able to show the world the necessity of the provision and their intention.

Your immediate family is very essential to the level of your performance in term of making the world to be in the light of the intention. The contribution of immediate family, extended family and relative are very essential to make a way ahead. One must learn on how to be very interactive and accommodating to make the family members to have interest in you and your need to be present in their midst. Human relationship is very relatively required to achieve things in life. I am not saying there are not some individuals without human relationship that excel, but they are minority compares with the others that fine tuned their cordial relationship to excel. So, the relationship issue is very crucial at the point of given consideration to the height of excelling or crossing over to the stage of no limitation.

Friend should be the best selling avenue for services and products. No wonder it is always said that, it is better to have the whole world as friends than being selective. Your friends are very crucial at the point of coming forth with a significant assignment and function. They are meant to be easily approached and persuaded, and as a result of this, they can be the axis of disseminating the ideas to the total world because they are as well connected with the other friend that you do not know. To then determine where should be the market for your services and products, it will be very worthwhile to mention your friends. If each of the so called friends can pick up the interest in what you do, there will be no doubt of you moving ahead to capture the entire world.

Being in a particular environment connotes that you have people around you. Apart from your immediate friends, being in good relationship with those who live around you is very cogent to be able to move ahead. Most of the ideas have been exterminated just because of no good relationship with the people around. The set of the individuals that are meant to use the services and products of your concern can not but be counted very important to have a completion in our view or anticipation. You must be able to understand the need to have them to have a completed nature of marketing or attainment of purpose.

If the primary assignment at the worship centers is just praying and going back home or the spiritual aspect of life without cordial unity to take a step ahead to understand what others want materially and physically, it might implies that the worship is not yet matured enough. It is very pertinent to give the full consideration to the things of heaven, mostly at the hour of prayers and intercession. But sincerely, without having the evident of the spirituality in the physical, it might be considered of oneself yet not to attain a meaningful result. If one can not be useful to the world in holistic, it is very pivot to be relevant to the associate in his doctrine pattern. To however illustrate with the issue of religious places, your marketing strategy should cut across the religion place you attend. Though, the marketing of your commodity must never be able to outweigh your primary objective which is to serve God, but there is no way you will serve God without serving humanity and you will have a completed life because God is in the humanity and His presence in the humanity must be accordingly noted and served to serve God. Marketing your service and commodities might even be more useful to the church not to talk of the body of the religion or the other congregation or members. Therefore, your marketing logic must be far away from the external individuals all alone, but must be extended to the immediate people around you in which your religion place and others are not exempted.

The issue of personal development is very worth taken. To ascend from a height to a greater height, there is always requirement of personal improvement and development. Improvement and development can only be noticed or accessed when one is well prepared and involved in the activities that lead to it. One of the major activities that give the quest for improvement however is personal interest in what it entails to make it reality. To be mixed and mingled with the various set of individuals with different opinion and mind set that can stand as the catalyst to the translation of life either willingly or unwillingly, there is every requirement to be involved in the training and the kind of the environment that can expand knowledge and foresight. However, at this point, one must be well prepared to share his view with the others too, to persuade them or urge them to key into what you do. Do not be surprised that the nature of the services and production you are engaged with is such that someone that you will call his attention to it is waiting for. And to be frank, the set of the individuals with various foresight and intention might be the very best of the individuals that can make vision to be reality and to be greatly updated. Therefore, sharing your intention and vision with the others at the point of adding value to yourself and what you know either formally or informally is very expedient and quite worth noted to move ahead or to accomplish vision.

To cut the story short, the world at large is wide enough to make what you have noted to be demonstrated. There is nothing within human capacity that is not useful. Those ideas and thought are hidden in you to make difference in your little capacity, but they can not be felt not until they are used accordingly and applied for the purpose that they are meant to fulfill. Therefore, we must strife add and compete with all factors that can lead us to our destiny and the essence of creation.

A very crucial aspect that can not be left untouched at the point of marketing products and services is the issue of ascertaining what happens to the products, materials and services that are not marketed. There are a lot of the adverse effects on the services and products not marketed. To quickly move through them, I will like to mention few, but might not be able to have a comprehensive illustration on them.

Without a full marketing, one might pass through the instance of experiencing stale products. It simply implies that, when one fails to invest time or exert his strength to what he has in plan to do, or what he has produced, such intention, services and products can be staled and outdated. Things change in line with the changes in life. The best of the product today might not be the best of that of tomorrow. Take for an illustration, the nature or kind of the vehicles that ruled years back are presently outdated and obsolete. If the production or sets of productions were not sold at when due, they will definitely be obsolete and outdated. This as well is applicable to the issue of services and consumable items.

The services and products might be hidden and unknown for years till they attain the stage of their deletion. There is always the need to have all what it takes to make the products and services well known at the very due session and time for their consumption. As said earlier, there is no purposeful idea and intention that is not vital to the issue of life when they are well placed and made known to the people that are meant to consume them. Therefore, there is extreme need of making the services and products available when due not to be hidden or unidentified by the set of individuals that have the mind set to consume them.

The issue of being obsolete can not be over emphasized as one of the major issues on the inability to market the products and services. I mentioned something ahead about being staled. Being staled leads the products and services to the stage of obsolete.

There will not be any meaningful reasoning in having services and products that can not perform their projected function. Therefore, there is always as a matter of need and urgency to project the nature of services and production towards the essential needs to be effective and functional. When the services and production are not working in alignment with their intention, they are made to be ineffective and purposeful and thereafter turn to a waste. Marketing makes the services and production to be at their best use.

When none is available to consume what you have, it will definitely leads to the lower in the interest or the production and provision of the services. Low production or activeness might not be able to create the profitability level of expectation. To however be availed with the opportunity of having better production and rendition of services, there is need to study the marketing strategies excessively and to be able to key into it accordingly.

There is something called economic of scale. These are the benefits you derive in what you do as a result of large purchase of raw materials or large production. Continuous and large production avail the producer or service provider to enjoy the higher economic of scale which then affect the efficiency of such business, the productivity and foresight.

When things are not moving on as expected, there is every tendency of having a set back, depression and discouragement. When the encouraging values are not involved anymore, the provision of the activities tends to be inactive and weakened. The service provider and producer must have what it entails to have the zeal to perform their best.

Another menace that inactiveness of marketing can cause is the issue of extermination or extinction. When the services and product are not demanded, it turns out to the inability to carter for the required resources to engage with the provision of service and production.

Conclusively here, inability to market accordingly might lead to the inability to perform optimally. To be in control of oneself or to be responsible for one's life, what he does must be well understood and have directional purpose that can make the end result of the intention to reach the final destination. When there is no enabling structure and efficacy to continue or to enjoy the benefits of the service rendition and productivity, there will definitely be an impediment to have a successful completion of projection or to optimally be in full utilization of resources and ideas.

However, to quickly go through the issues that might likely make one to be inactive during the cause of marketing, I will quickly enumerate them as follows;

- The rigor of marketing
- Means of publicity and marketing
- Nature of product and services
- Responsiveness of the market audience
- Availability of raw materials
- Availability of resources and tools and associated materials
- Electrification provision
- Interest and level of endurance
- Closeness to the market
- Accessibility or nearness to the road network
- Enough capital to set up and to move around
- Availability of the market or people in need of such products and services
- Inexperience and lack of full technical know how or acumen of the vision
- Being pessimistic and lack of courage
- Economic, political and social unrest
- Inadequate availability of transportation
- Too much of competitors
- Importation
- Interest of the populace on the imported commodities and service, e.t.c

Some people tend to question them selves of how long should marketing be done. It should be done on daily basis as a result of interest in what one does. It implies that the availability or in-availability of product and services might not be able to change the position of marketing if the interest is still very aligned with the intention and vision at the inception. Marketing is a continuous phase of the business intention. It is the breathing system of any business in consideration.

To end this chapter, I must reiterate that marketing is as expedient as the business if one needs to have an exclusive feedback, result and remark. Also, there is no way one can be in charge or be responsible for his life without being able to manage the core region and expedient part of life which is marketing of personal worth, services and production.

Chapter Eleven(11)

<u>COMPETE WITH YOURSELF</u>
<u>INTERNALLY</u>

To have what it entails to be responsible for one's life, there are numerous things that are essential and various vital roles that must be played by the individuals along side with their motive. Competing with oneself internally is a very necessary aspect of being responsible for one's life that must be examined to detail. There is none that has nothing important to do, but not all can recognize the important things that live in them. The internal inspiration generates the heat to produce a certain outcome or the other. What a man can see can never be forgotten to be mentioned or addressed at the point of evaluating its potency and what he can accomplish accordingly. Without seeing anything, there might not be room to accomplish extensively, because the urge and the drive to take control of the objective might not be available in him.

As human being, we must have a particular issue that we are bordered with, and such issue must be the core point of exerting our strength. To be responsible for one's life, there must be internal forces that prompt a man to do a certain thing or the other. There must be something that a man runs after to accomplish as a result of his motive to be made or to be optimally created. If nothing is in a man to take him around, irrelevant things will take him over to where he is not meant to be.

Struggling with the internal contents is needed to be able to settle for a purpose or attain a dream. You have what you can see, I have what I can see and everyone has something or the other to see. Therefore, to have the series of the developmental agenda and output or favourable responses to the amelioration of the issues of life, there is need to see something that can make significance in your contribution. The magical translation of what can be seen to the activities that makes one's contribution implies vision. Without cleared vision, there can never be cleared destiny.

I have said it time without number, the essence of competition should not be based on the kind of competition that has to do with the fellow human beings, but must be a replica of the competition that are lured with one's purpose to make a vision inclusively noted while one lives. There is something that must be competed with and struggle with internally, else, the essence of having a fulfilling life might be unattained. Fighting with the people around you can never be what makes your life worthwhile, but fighting with your internal vision and looking into how they can be structured to fight for you or to introduce you accordingly.

It is very possible to live for ages without being able to have any substantial identification of purpose. Many have lived their lives without the capability of being able to actualize any part of their vision. Their visions were made to be dreams all through or sometimes, they get to know of the need to demonstrate them lately when they are incapacitated. The book is relating on the massive requirement of the important segment of being responsible to one's life as a result of his ability to identify his vision and to work with it accordingly. Without having what it entails to be made or being so intelligent to affiliate with the sources of inspiration that instigates one's passion to be at full use to create a future that is worth while or of concern to the necessary places of their functionality, one might never be where he should be all through his living. Digging deep to determine your area of essentiality is quite demanding to have a nature of life that is very complete and competitive. However, the requirement to have something that you can see but which no other one can see to be an exceptional and unique individual.

Having a self challenging attitude is also a chief consideration of the thought towards competition with oneself internally. If at all you are not bordered or moved by any other thing in life, what you can see should be able to move you. There must be internal competition to the tune of challenging yourself and asking yourself series of question that should lead you to your destination or to actualize your vision. Some people live life of no challenges, which simply implies that, they may have nothing to contend with. There is maximum need to have an assignment created within for yourself or a vision that should make you to work out the magic and dynamics in you. Without having a due pressure that drags your internal component to the height of functionality, there might not be factors that are responsible for such action. Something must be responsible for the instigation of the move that brings about commitment to the activities that create concepts for achievement, and that must be the priority of everyone to have yielding and effective resources to multiply and convert the chances to the opportunities.

However, there is no way a vision can be run without the full participation of the individual. There is no one without something significant to do in life, but not everyone usually get set to be involved in the activities that should usher them to the height of recognition and stage of full acceleration and performance. When a vision is separated from the person that has the vision, the vision is secluded of the pilot phase and idea. There might be ideas that were given at the inception, but better to have the real owner of the idea available to be of assistance and to give the brief of the whole logics of the vision from time to time. There must not be separation of the logics and its source to have unique outcome. The body must not run around with the intention of accomplishment without the due consideration of what the inner mind is passing to it. The mind or inner man and the entire component must be able to work in synergy to have a complete or adequate outcome.

The series of the activities that a man passes through are the most valuable of the factors that upgrade them. To be well upgraded in thought and scope, there is always the need to be able to pass through series of the issues around you. Most individuals run away from issues instead of them to get more insight therein, there is no way a man can be intimidated of the issues around him, and he will be availed the grace to multiply. Human nature of multiplicity is based on the level of their involvement in the daily activities, but so painful that most of the human fail to understand the importance therein. To be able to set a higher standard for oneself, he must never be a complaining minded or someone that takes delight in the flimsy excuses around, but be committed to the involvement that can provoke the internal person to set a higher standard. Most of the activities around were made as a result of the mind set to conquer. Therefore, the mind to rule over the activities must be the major concern of human projection and endeavor to create a yard stick that is worthwhile and standard enough.

Similarly, there is always the quest to be an evaluator to the level of success or failure of oneself if he actually wants to compete with himself internally. Not everyone gives attention to the right things because they are not made to evaluate the worth of the secretion of their intuition and how their mind functions. The inner human being keeps on talking to us when an action is got right or wrong, but only few individuals administer the justice or admit to the judgment to change. One should constantly be involved in the activities that consider the impact of his action to be able to understand better of the tricks that are meant to be implemented to have a better decision and undertakings or withdraw from such act.

The competition must be very constructional and impactational to end up the internal forces to be outstanding and expedient in nature. At the point you compete with yourself in relation to your concern and intention, such intention must be genuine and of humanity concern to be taken to add up additional value to the components of the varieties of the opportunities around. At the phase of competing with oneself internally, there is always the need to realize that, any competition of any kind that is not to the improvement and increment of the existence is just a mere waste. To be constructional means that one is fully loaded with the activities that should be a catalyst to the fulfillment of your destiny and at the same time standing as the measure of influence to the society and the world in holistic. Being constructional makes one to be wide enough to see the need to be inclusive in the scope that takes the world to the higher ground. It gives the internal and external components the strength that is meant to be well nurtured to have a full completeness of their actions.

To be responsible in all facets of lives, there is always the requirement to be moved by what one can see.

There is no doubt that seeing something relevant in life is a matter of importance of life and as important as the creation that revolves around the intention. One must be able to have a deep thought that is solid enough to be a catalyst for the formation of the stronger desire for the ambition and intention. What one sees is quite separated from what one is told or the information that is extracted from a source or the other. The conviction in what you can see however stands to be the ultimate potency to the drive to accomplish a set object. Seeing something means seeing everything about your thought which others might not be able to see in a similar manner. In the same vein, that what you can access or see is essential, the drive to mention them to the world or demonstrate them can never be understated or made to be irrelevant in value. What can be seen are the things that are formed to be the basis for the foresight and one's faith. What one can see is the table that enlisted the various program and gets them well schedule for their implementation. There is vital need to be able to be affixed accordingly with the logics around the dream and vision, and to have the total preparedness to have their full execution.

Chapter Twelve (12)

<u>BE DUTIFUL AND GENUINE</u>

Being dutiful means being engaged willingly or having the feeling and interest to be functional in term of disregarding the limitable influences to be creative enough to have something worthwhile to be accomplished. There is need for one to have the feeling to be involved in the series of the activities that leads to a certain result or the other. The other synonyms that are interrelated with word are; obedient, well behave, responsive, submissive, loyal, e.t.c. There can never be any activities that can be created without the interest of the men, and sincerely, the interest all alone is not the major concern but being able to make a composition and willingness to be involved in the series of the items to the connection that paves an avenue for the activities that make provision for the interests or values. Dutiful minded are self motivated and self moved in the sense that, their precepts and ideology are loaded with the virtue and the core unbeatable dramatic zealous demonstrating potency that make them to be freely involved or act accordingly with the little of the effort around them. Most of the industries and organization could not attain their set objectives just because of the disposition of the staff in their attempt not to be well represented where they are needed. Dutiful minded are always of the zeal to have a meaningful contribution in the midst of nothing, they share the motive and the vision of the organization and the industries in which they work with the organization. They are always handling things around the interest of the entity they represent as their own and making the conditions around the development of the organization of their interest and maximum concern. A dutiful minded has all what it takes him to begin and to continue even when there is no result or surplus of outcome on what he does. They are always of the philosophy of making it to take place with the little effort or no effort of the others. They have what it takes to change the situation around them willingly and to interpret the basic facts that should change the odds situation to favourable and interesting one.

Without being dutiful, there might be only few or no activities in the world. The dutiful minded are the initiator of the ideas, they make the ovation to be loud and set a different paste on the ball game. They are always making the world to have the experience and feeling that, there are too many numerous things that are meant to be actualized and to be completed from time to time to have the nature of the balancing that must make the world to be in her best state. Dutiful minded are the determinant of the future of the world in the sense that, they are always well prepared and of the mind set to make things that are reasonable to take their position, which then means that, the negative influences are as well noted and considered before they emanate. Dutiful minded make moves that translates the condition around to the best option to living and create a conducive environment that habours a perfect existence of humanity. Dutiful minded makes the hidden potential appearing and exhibited to the tune of recreating the created ideas and creating the uncreated for the intention of allowing their motive to move the world to rest or peaceful arena and destination. They are always developing their internal innate capacity with no effort or little of the effort. This is because they are optimally involved before they are either introduced or shown the reason for them to be available for the intention or situation that requires their participation. When one looks into the internal composition and talents, he means the potential or skills that are formed internally. Therefore, to have a dutiful minded, these sets of all internal components are expedient to be at work freely and expressly without even thinking of the quantification of the derivable benefits. They make all their qualities and characteristics to be of importance to the world enlargement and increment.

On the other hand, being genuine has to do with the reality aspect of living. It has to do with who someone is without being mixed or diluted with any artificial impetus. Actually, there is no way a man can be represented as who he is not, and sincerely, if at all, mistaken, he is identified as what he is not, who he is will surely be rightly exhibited as and when due. Genuine personality has to do with the attribute of a man. It has to do with his techniques and tactics towards the related issues of life. It has to do with the functional effect a man has over his environment. It can be said to be the real exhibition of thought and action to make difference in one's little capacity or horizon.   The related words are; indisputable, authentic, real, indubitable, undeniable, uncontrovertibly, e.t.c.

In line with the thought, I am of the opinion that, demeanor and conduct must be regular and steady as a matter of reasoning to add up authentic impact in the creation of the environment in which they are enclosed. There must never be fluctuation or instability to the behavioural pattern that is projected to making sure that there is a conclusive end result, most especially in the world which should be the major concern of all to experience peace and unity in diversity and coexistence.

However, to merge the thought together at the point of being well set to be responsible for one's life, there is always the need to be involved in the activities around. There are thousands of the activities that are revolving the world of the men and around their living, there is always the ultimate need to at all times create the opportunity that can bring them to a certified issues that should make them to be well involved and to genuinely take control. Taking control however should not be based on the consideration of what the people have to say or the reaction of men to the inspiring moves that should make the world to have a better advantage.

Readiness to be part and parcel of the option to the greatness is not a choice but a necessity. To attain the stage of no limitation, there is utmost necessity of individuals to make contributions. One must be fully set to be involved and to make a simple input. Most of the men that often say that they have nothing to give or to contribute are always the reverse of their saying. I have thousands of friends that have said that they do not have the flare or interest in teaching because they are often intimidated or shy of the conglomeration of individuals, but eventually, either willingly or not, they became one, but they often perform better than the former teaching personnel. What I am saying is that, the mind set to be involved to make simple impact can not be exempted at the point of generating the value that should translate the world to the best of the nature of the standard that can avail opportunity to the world. Therefore, one must be well ready and set to pick up a simple option of being available to inject value in his quota to define his destiny and being in full control of the world in his own capacity.

Another very viable content that defines a dutiful minded and genuine personality is the attitude of being able to make a function to occur when there is none. As a dutiful person and individual, counting on the function around might never be the very best of your option to be made, but having the mind to have a function even when there is none in existence. Creating of a function in your capacity to make a functional output is one of the major criterions for the dutiful mind to be associated with. Without the creation of the function that are not available around and the activities that generate the economic functionalities, there might not be one. Therefore, the need to be functional and productive to be a creator of activities other than relying on the created activities which might not be there by the way if not struggled for such.

Being a man of responsibility and one that directs the affairs of his life entails one to be able to think above the impossibilities and short coming. Many decisions are dashed as a result of the impediments that most of them have experienced and passed through. There is definitely nothing impossible when one is set to accomplish such motive. The unattainable activities are such that are not of the interest to the humanity. There is always a way out on any form of issues, because the issues point out the relative solution when they are critical examined and cross checked. Therefore, as a dutiful and genuine man, there is need to have the focus on the possibility of life to be outstanding and successful.

The aspect of living above what can be seen with the literal sight or ordinarily is very essential to get to the stage of no limitation at the point of becoming the real owner of his destiny or passionate to be responsible in life. Most of the things that are physical are temporary and they have their expiration time. But things that are not seen but live at the realm higher than physical are often very dependable when you can discover the actual need to tap into them to make a viable environment or to contribute to the notable activities around the world.

Thinking of taking the lead is also an important phase of being dutiful and genuine. There are thousands of the issues that do not require too much of effort to control or adjust in the world, but they are never accomplished as a result of not having someone that should take a lead. The leaders are the great influential individuals in the world. They are the risk taker and they tend to make a move to eradicate or bring to an end the difficulties and deformities in the world as a whole. Leaders do not consider what they will gain or benefit in the whole logics around their demonstration of ideas and undertakings, but they consider the benefit of the others first to take their influential action. To be a leader, one must be able to see beyond ordinary or the set of the issues around, but must be able to think and take action that should ameliorate the tensed situation and improper event that live with human beings. To then show oneself as a dutiful and genuine being or individual, one of the most important attribute which is taken the lead must never be found wanting or not part of such human nature.

There must be attractiveness and willingness to have pleasure in the activities around. To be dutiful means the mind that has interest in the activities around it. Without the passion and the wiling act to be part of the activities that occur around you, one might never be able to see the actual place of his necessity and involvement. An indolent minded and lazy one might never see the reason for them to be involved in the activities around them. And sincerely, being industrious and hard working is a reality on the path to make a realistic outcome. Therefore, being dutiful is an act of being passionate to do work or contribute in your capacity to have influence in the world. Taking action that leads the world ahead in the major issue at the point of attractiveness and willingness must be well taken into consideration to have a dutiful minded taking up their responsibility around their life's issues.

Checking through what can distinct you or separate you from the populace or the crowd is one of the important aspects of life that is required of the dutiful mind and a thorough individual. To be a master of your destiny and to be responsible indeed, there is always the need to be well involved in the things that has to do with distinctiveness or exclusiveness. Without being able to work around those things that are exceptional, dramatic and amazing, there might never be any way out or excelling avenue to glory. Glory will be impaired and refrained because of the fact that, what should separate one is not available or exhibited.

Be free and give freely what you have to give to make contribution. There is no one that does not have something exceptional, but not everyone knows the need to exhibit the values. To find a direct measure towards the genuine contribution and making the full impact, there must be connection with what you have and how you give them. Without your willingness to give what you have freely or to be absolutely free indeed to have a meaningful influence, there might never be an avenue to the real establishment and growing of purpose. Therefore, to be dutiful means being willing to give freely and be free with one environment, and being willing to have a full control over his destiny.

There is always the need to show concern in a positive way and at a positive angle at the point of making your contribution. Any contribution that does not have a positive inclination must never be tolerated to rule your destiny. A man that is of full purpose and intention to have a full degree of measure of achieving his destiny or being at the helm of having full charge on his life must be willing and at the same time show concern on the positive strategies and system that should lead the world to the height of better value and honour.

Doing whatever you want to do with perfection and genuinely is very pivot to have a dutiful minded individual. There is a statement and saying that says whatever worth doing at all is worth doing well. There is always value in connection with what one does, and the value must never be made to be devalued or degraded as a result of any significant or insignificant element around it. To have a responsible life and being in custody of one's destiny, there is always the very need to be available for the perfection in dealing and endeavors. You are better defined with what you do or engaged with, because they are often better travelled than you. Therefore, to be well represented and to be fully defined to the others, there must be description and proper illustration of you and your work. This as a matter of fact, counts plenteously on the level of your responsibility and the value of your destiny. To then however have all it takes to be made or to be responsible for your life, there must be thorough decision on being a perfectionist and a discipline minded.

Chapter Thirteen (13)

<u>BOLDNESS, COURAGE AND FAITH TO SUCCEED</u>

We are still on the issues that revolve around determination of destiny and being responsible accordingly. As a human being, there are numerous factors that are very necessary, and they are a must to be complied with before a reasonable responsibility can be resolved to. It is very easy to say that you have a trait or the other in you which are of various kinds of your interest, but better said than being done. There are lots of talent and traits that are never active as a result of the low level of their consideration and attention. When some of the necessary traits are lost or not available for their respective functions, there will definitely be gap and inactiveness to make a discrete decision.

One of the factors to be considered as regards this book is however the boldness, courage and faith to succeed. Without boldness or courage and faith, there might never be an avenue to greatness or achieving destiny. I said earlier that all vision can be accomplished but not all will definitely be accomplished because many of the destinies are not well prepared for to manifest. It is only the destiny that one is well prepared to accomplish that is relevant to its objective. There is quest to have success at all cost as a result of discovery if actually one is set to doing so. These words will be defined and well illustrated before I move ahead.

Boldness is a habit that makes one to press on in the midst of instability and storm. It is an act of making a decision and consistency in such decision till they manifest. It is an act commitment till the very ending of a vision. It means making out possibilities around the impossibilities of the world. It means living for certainty in the midst of uncertainty of living. It means looking for the best alternative to suppress pressure and the inconsistencies that rule the situation and condition around human nature. Boldness means; valor, daring, courage, bravery, e.t.c. These are the attributes that are reserved for the set of the individuals that are inclined with the nature of the attribute that make them not to be swerving or interrupted in any form to accomplish their motive.

Being bold or courageous means moving ahead in spite of rugged nature associated with the relevance of living. It means seeing the right results and brave outcomes when others can not or might not see their essence for the intention of demonstrating their values and making influences. Boldness has to do with a broaden mind and heart that could see above the superstitious realm to do the right thing or carry out a function. It is a nature of activities that determine the strength and conviction. It has to do with how rugged and intentional someone is, and how he can make his vision to be materialized or accomplished. It determines what one sees and the reason to give dying attitude to cause it to manifest. It means increase in innate composition to the attainment in the midst of suppression and depression. It is an alternative to failure and impossibilities in life.

However faith on the other hand is the perception and conviction that transcend its immediate result. It can be said to be a reasoning that expresses an intention to be accomplished even though they are yet to be embarked on. These are the series of attempts that take their stand in the condition of achieving of the set objectives or foresight before they are experienced or worked on. It is said to be a full execution and completion of a project even when they are yet to be experimented and attained. However, to be rightly placed and to be stationed at the point of achievement and to be responsible for one's life accordingly, there is an extreme need to have the faith and to be courageous.

To be the master of life and to be responsible, all you do must be well analyzed and freely administered. Your intention must be demonstrated without exhibiting any form of fear or timidity to have a better performance, and when there is timidity and fear, they must never be in control or constitute devastating action that should not make value to be relevant and intention to be accomplished. Courage and faith must work hand in hand to bring purpose to completeness.

Believing in yourself is also very relevant to making your vision to be attained and to have the full responsibility. The courage and faith are the things of the mind or internal components which must have its origin right away from the inward part of a man. This can however be possible when the mind is with the full preparedness to work with the objective or function slated. However, to be strong enough to have a responsibility and to be in charge of destiny, one must be adequate enough to have belief to introduce him to the full performance and execution without having any form of fear.

There is always an issue or the other, and issues can never be completely resolved because of the nature of the series of the issues are coming up from time to time, and sincerely, they are never similar in nature. This is just the reason why the issue resolved yesterday might not be resolved in the same vein today, and that of today might not be resolved the same way that as that of yesterday. Issues are often the directory to the series of the activities that leads to success. When a man is possessed with the skill of identifying the issues around him, he is prone to having a faster movement to accomplishment and to move ahead in his intention and projection. However, issues are meant to be resolved amicably when one is courageous and having the faith on the possibilities. Seeing beyond the issues around you however is very relevant to be able to have the kind of preparation that can be an assisting factors to having solution and remedy to it. Hence the essence of the courage and faith to work concurrently to deliver the set objective and vision that is assigned to a specific project.

I said something in the previous chapter as regards self reliance and independence. There is crucial need to be very independence and self reliance to get some things done or actualized. And without the due courage and boldness with faith as part of you or your nature, there might be witty consideration of achievement and actualization of purpose. Being free to a certain level matters at the point of carrying out some activities that are meant to be the structure to an enviable development and an outstanding performance. It is never a child's play to create a condition that can allow you grow or having a responsive decision to your vision when occupied with a certain thing or the other. But it takes a full courage and faith to outlive the nature of the cumbersome type of the condition that stands as regulator of one's decision or as deterrent to the actualization of one's objective. To be responsible and be accelerated to the tune of being fully in control of the activities around you and to be the right owner of your destiny, there is essentiality of being independent and self reliance.

Another thing that must be very structurally identified and understood is the issue of the thin line between the success and failure. To be responsible for one's life or to have the absolute control over the activities that surrounds him to create other opportunities that can bring the opportunities around closer to one's finger tip, one must be able to attain a conclusion that, only thin line separates the two circumstances that might require similar effort to attain. Thinking on the boldness, courage and faith has to do with the things that one has the absolute permission and order to covert to advantages. It has to do with either looking for the avenue to win or to lose. Wining or losing in the race of life is as a result of choice, and the choice that one embarks on really matters on the actual outcome that he arrives eventually. The understandability of the two natures of outcome are however very relevant at the point at which one is cross examining the direction and the conclusive motive in life. Studying the thin line and the ability to understand that, the choice either makes you the first choice or another is very critical and answerable at the point of arriving at the projected destination. The thin line between the success and the failure must be well outlined and critically peruse to have the choice to decide on the path and the direction to follow as human being.

When there is nothing, there must be something to be caught up with to create things that should lead a man ahead. Without seeing what is relevant to take one ahead or to see the need to execute an idea, there might never be any reason to achieve such idea. To be a better representative of one's idea, one must have caught up with a definite reason to make such view achievable. What each man sees are very relevant at the point of given what they have to make impact. There might never be any access to the vast outcome without seeing what you can see clearly and making provision for how best they can be to be clearly established. Things that are established are caused as a result of the capability of investing on what can be seen and having a directional course on how best they can be demonstrated. Therefore, having the real sense of belonging to the achieving of the purpose is not but a mandatory to the instance of having something special and relevant to attain at the course of having nothing or something to do.

The attributes stated as part of being responsible for one's life can not but be part of attempting undertakings and values with purpose. A man that knows the reason to be bold, courageous and full of faith must be able to attempt all undertakings and values with intention that is more than mere execution. To be bold means to be unswerving in the attempt to make a meaningful contribution or to act to achieve a particular intention. It has to do with the radical establishment of purpose, expression and logics. It must do or go with the necessary factors that encourage the internal efficacy to react or act in a particular way or the other. It is an expression of confidence and authority to act accordingly either with permission or not. But it is necessary to state it that, in a structured environment, permission is required either expressly or implicitly. To however study the needs to have a completeness nature of life, one might not be able to have a true nature of end result without looking into the aspect of being purposeful and directional.

Lastly, to discuss on boldness, courage and faith, there is extreme importance on relating on the success or failure before they emanate. The attribute that sees beyond the boundary and limit of operational standard, that creates a result and successful outcome before the true nature of the outcome comes around is the point to be examined. There is always the need to be able to have an overview of what the end result of an activity should be before their commencement. The position of one's mind to have a successful outcome as regards his action or inaction is very crucial to make the eventual decision or outcome. Success or failure is a must to be seen before their time of manifestation. One must be able to know if the decision embarked on is necessary to be undertaken or not prior its time of manifestation. There should be a conclusive position to see the very last from the beginning of the action.

However, these enumerated factors are substantial to be associated with the issues of boldness, courage and faith towards having a thorough responsibility and

being in full control of oneself as the case might be on
the track of hijacking one's destiny.

Chapter Fourteen (14)

<u>EXECUTE THINGS THAT ARE SELF DEFENSIVE</u>

I will quickly go through the sub topic briefly in its context to the responsibility of life and being in control of destiny. To be able to have the full responsibility and to take full direction and gain full control on the destiny, involving in the things that are self defensive is very compulsory. One should be able to define and to defend his action and inaction on each attempt on the activities he is prone to. As said initially, there is no action that does not have its conclusive aspect before they are taken. At the point of demonstrating this action however, there is need to be able to evaluate the intention critically, to have the full understanding of what it entails and what products has it to add as value or its reverse. All action must be defensive in the sense that, one should be able to analyze the logics behind such action at the point of having the need to interpret their essence. An action that does not have a spectacular intention is an action that should never be taken. Such actions that come ordinarily this way are representative of the cluelessness and abnormality.

There are several things that occur without purpose or voluntarily without the mind set to have them, just by circumstance, but most of the actions are regulated by the projection of the men. However, if there is need for an action to be effective and to be administered, then there must be a tangible reason for it.

To be able to have the self defensive part of execution, one must be able to get familiar and acquitted with the do and do not of life. What do I mean by this, there are some certain things that are not expected of a human to be engaged with in life, most especially in relation with the others, one must be guided and be very careful about such issues. Also, there are some things that very essential for one to be involved with while alive, such operations must not be counted wanting or left undone. Showing compassion to the others, creating ways and opportunities for the others when due, responsibility for the initiation of the ideas that should lead to development, leaving a legacy of doing the right things, extending of affection to the needy and those who might be in need of your support, thinking of the others first, living in peace with all men, e.t.c. are very essential as a human being to be quality that should make his disposition and values. To then be responsible for one's life, there is essentiality of these values to be noted. There are some things that when they are not considered or examined in one's life, they might be hindrance to the activities that lead to responsibility of oneself to doing things that are self defensive. Such things are very important to be well looked into never to be at a cross junction or unable to justify them at the point at which they are meant to be interpreted to the world.

Going further, to have a self defensive on the related matters that constitutes responsibility to life or taking full control of destiny, the constructive pattern and ideology of dealing with the executables must be well understood and clearly defined. Without being able to understand the structure of an idea clearly at the point of executing them, there might be confusion at the moment of making the world to understand them. Understanding how thought and activities around the frame work of the executables are composed is very relative to the presentation and representation of its purpose. The in depth understanding of what one embarks on is very necessary to be able to have the detailed knowledge that can make his dealings and actions well elucidated or explain when the need be. There is no action that has no structure or basis, the basis are very compulsory to be well understood and properly digested to be able to attend to the issues around the cause of such action and activities that instigates such reasons.

When one is trying to look into the self defensive aspect of life, one is looking into the area that has to do with the correlation of what one does and his vision. There must be correlation between what one does and his vision to be indeed a defensive minded. When what one does is separated from his vision or what he says, it become tragedy in the sense that, it implies that one entity is simultaneously working on the same issue oppositely, which might be the greatest hazard or institutionalizing of the different ideas to make a whole. One must be well composed and out-rightly coordinated to make a responsibility attainable. Any responsibility that has not value of having correlation between the vision and action however turns out to be the most miserable at the moment of defense.

Being natural really matters to be able to attain the greatest deed and to be self defensive in the activities around one's intention. When one tries to be oneself, he can see clearly what he is meant to be and going through the systems that should make his opinion to be reckoned with is structured like to his vision. He knows better of the dichotomy of both the action and inaction that brings out his best. Being able to be self reliance is a major constitute of the aspect that leads to the self defense. Defensive action can only take place when one put into the consideration the area that has to do with self reliance. The adequacy in the empowerment of the nature of the inbuilt characteristics to formulate the true idea without being an imitator of another is however very necessary to generate the basis for the proper responsibility which can not be separated from being a man of one's intention.

Chapter Fifteen (15)

<u>ACT AS IF YOU HAVE EVERYTHING</u>

As I conclude gradually on the relevant circumstances that are very necessary to be opportune the diversified benefits at the paste of being solely responsible for the issues of life and to be in charge of one's destiny, I will like to wrap my analogy up with the possession of the attitude that one has everything to make his vision accomplished, even where there is nothing. The major barrier of not being able to accomplish a task should not be described in its impossibilities as regards not attempting or given priority to chances that leads to success. There are some hidden skill and potential that are very inactive not until they are forced to be operational. Take for an example; if someone suddenly pushes you towards an opening of a reasonable length, without any one telling you to jump with all your strength, your innate person prompts you to doing so, which eventually might lead to jumping over the gap. But to say that you should jump ordinarily, you might not be able to do that. There was a day I was coming from the Lagos Island to Mainland which was approximately 1,100 km distance. I never had the plan to trek the distance, but the circumstance compel me to doing so. Getting to the bus stop, I discovered that the traffic was almost moving into the offices. It was a stand still, no movement day. Prior to my coming, I was told some vehicle were on the spot for hours which was eventually confirmed authentic when I joined the queue. I was on my foot for more that 2 hours without any vehicle moving an itch. This however triggered my adrenalin to kick into the action to decide to trek it. Sincerely, it takes a vehicle on high speed to spend 10 minutes to cover the distance, but I must confess to you that, I did not know the time the journey was completed.

At the point of the beginning of the journey, there was preparedness to embark on it, and the mind was fully set to have it takes place without minding the shortcomings that might be faced on the road. In such a way that this journey was scheduled, life is meant to be as well scheduled in such manner, minding not the predicament, but be mindful of the ups and down that might erupt as the journey commences. Acting as if one has everything when there is nothing means that one has already completed the intention from within before the commencement of such intention, it means that, the end has been deduced right away from the beginning of an action which facilitates the easiness in looking at the obstacles very quite less complex to resolve when they emanate.

Possibility is an element of the mind. And it must be well demonstrated within before the actualization of purpose or agenda that should translate to the fulfillment of intention. Things that are of the mind are never can be seen with naked eyes, but they can be well executed for the world to see at when due and their manifestation time period. Seeing the best result and the materialistic aspect of life that should propel the efficacy of a man to actualize the prepared objective is quite very relevant within before their moment of actualization. Hence, there is no way that one can be fully responsible for his life or be in charge of his destiny without having the full consideration of the possibility which must be developed from the mind.

When all things are vanished, one must be able to conclude that all things are available. The end of a journey should begin another one instantly without any flimsy excuse. There is not anything like end of the road when one can see clearly the whole essence to the intention to be experimented. There can be end of a phase of a journey, but that does not mean that there is no alternative route to accomplish the projected vision when one can expend time on the measures to achievement. It is very possible someone has said that a certain thing or the other is not possible or can not be achieved, but I want you to know that, all what a man can see at the realm higher than physical are executable when the inner mind is fully set to assume the duty to make them to materialize.

On the other hand, being a determining minded and acting as if there is every provision for the solution of a certain mission has to do with the ability to convert the misfortune to fortune. What do I mean by this? The easiest avenue to have an edge way in life is to be able to determine the issues around and to be able to proffer the relative solution to them. There are thousands of the issues living with us and causing difficulties on daily basis on the conducive living of the human nature. These sets of the issues are meant to be critically analyzed and looked into to create within them the adjustment that can be the ameliorating values to the existence. Therefore, a man must be able to understand how these issues can be translated to the fortunes around, and to create an outstanding grade for the living in holistic.

The ability to see something higher than what others can see is another expensive feature that must be deliberated on to have completeness in the issue of having the dominion over destiny and being responsible accordingly. Anyone that is standing or looking at the avenue of looking into the matters as if they are not one, or thinking as if he has everything to make his decision accomplished must be able to see something that is above ordinary when others are seeing ordinary things. Seeing above the ordinary when others can only see what is ordinary is what will make you to have the inclination to be positive and to point out the whole essence of the need to have a mission accomplished. Without seeing it differently, you might not be able to see in difference with the others. The valuable difference between the perspective of viewing however emanates the embodiment of the feature that constitutes exceptionality and leading to outstanding execution of ideas and purpose.

At the point of acting as if you have everything to accomplish your purpose in life, you must never be indolent or irrelevant. It is very compulsory that one enjoys being involved in the series of the activities that should make the objective to come to conclusion. There might not be any magic that can work itself out without the thorough participation of the human. The participation and inclusion of the human is very relevant to the attainment of any decision. However, for one to be responsible, there is need to be participant in the activities that user him to his glory. One must move. Even to move what can not move or ordinarily will not move.

You may never be awaited of anyone to come over to push you into the action that should elevate you. There are some times that, one waits and luckily enough he sees someone to come to assist him to act on a certain vision, while many talents are being wasted as a result of inability to act accordingly when due. Looking into the possibility in life has to do with the ability to willingly move into an action that should lead to the apex of his purpose. There is no one that can not move ordinarily when there is interest in the vision or the assignment to be undertaken. Interest precedes the nature of move to make an accomplishment. One must be self motivated and driven to accomplish a purpose of any nature. This is one of the critical factors to the achievement of mission and to be responsible for the life relevant issues that has to do with the destiny in quote.

Thinking straight to accomplish in life is very expedient also to have a mind well set to act as if it has everything to accomplish all planned vision. Thinking straight does not mean that one should not have the second thought ones in a while, but the real thought of the intention should always subdue the negativities. Negative minded and reasoned individual might not be able to accomplish anything meaningful or see anything important in the little they have contributed to make an objective attained. There will always be advantages and disadvantages on various visions, but the ability to have a distinctive clarity on the need to have a certain idea implemented is quite very necessary at the point of having a fulfillment on a certain issue. Being cumbered with the negation can be responsible for being unable to make a genuine instance of positive influence. There is need to have the straight thinking overseeing the opulence in the various negation that might try to stand as impediment to accomplish.

Conclusively, to have a thorough responsibility and to gain the full control of one's destiny, there is need to be able to work or act decisively without minding the worst to come. I have to conclude this book by saying that, sometimes, things do not work as expected, but they can work when you are determined to create an enviable environment for them to work. There are thousands of the people that thought to be millionaire, but they are not till they died. It is never a curse or because they have not tried, but because they could not experiment their vision accordingly to the standard of the vision. If at all things do not go right, it does not mean that you are not doing anything, but you are not getting the right trick to make your vision working aright. When the logics and strategies that leads to vision is not conformed with that of the vision, things are set apart and vision are desolate. Therefore, having a vision that is not working does not count a man an indolent, but saying that the strategies must be upgraded to have a distinctive end result.

The issue of responsibility is very essential to be able to meet up with the standard yard stick of a bright destiny, hence, the need to give a thorough thought to the analysis and the discussion within the context of the book. Definitely, there must be one or two benefits that can be extracted in the book if it is well digested and examined. I am quite privileged to have a conclusion so fast on the relative issues to the factors that revolve around the human expectancy on the issues of responsibility to fashion greatness as the cause might be.